Lori,
Herstorically yours,
Sharon Kay Wood

Womanly yours,
Mabs Holcomb
3-15-90

DEAF WOMEN

A Parade through the Decades

Mabs Holcomb & Sharon Wood

DawnSignPress Berkeley, California

The information in this book is true and complete to the best of our knowledge. The
authors and publisher have made every effort
to accurately represent the lives of Deaf
women. We regret being unable to include
many outstanding Deaf women of the past as
well as the present.

Acknowledgments

We express our deep appreciation to mother Jo Ann E. Glasby Wood and to husband Roy, head of the Holcomb clan for their confidence and encouragement in this endeavor.

We are also greatly indebted to:

• Sally Auerbach, of New York, for suggesting that we merge our presentations (formal and entertaining) at the NAD convention in Baltimore, Maryland, in 1984. It was our first encounter.

• Roslyn Rosen for confidence in and inspiration for this project.

• Alexander Fleischman (Sports); Simon Carmel, Henry Buzzard and Bernard Sussman (Early Years); Agnes M. Padden (Gallaudet University); and Barbara Ray Holcomb, National Technical Institute for the Deaf (NTID) for their valuable assistance in providing leads for finding data for the book.

• Laurent Clerc Cultural Fund — Gallaudet University Alumni Association — for the grant-seed money.

• Gallaudet University Archives and Learning Resources Staff, especially Corrine Hilton, photo curator.

• Special thanks and love to Francis Higgins for sharing his papers on deaf women which he delivered at several banquets — in remembrance of his dear, late wife, Catherine Bronson Higgins.

• Many special THANKS to Kathleen Schreiber, George Attletweed, Ausma Smits, James Cartledge, Tina Jo Breindel, Joe Dannis, Ben Bahan, Tom Schlegal, and Bertt Lependorf for their criticisms and copy-editing — a labor of love.

• Lois Hoover, her sister, Carol, for design & production.

We also appreciate the many valuable contributions from friends of deaf women.

Yours for greater recognition of deaf women,

—*Mabs & Sharon*

TO ALL DEAF WOMEN IN AMERICA

New Horizons for Deaf Women

"Woman should be free as the air to learn what she will and to devote her life to whatever vocation seems good to her. . . . It is true that we have made a start in the right direction. But that start has been made very recently, and it is too early to pass sentence on the results."

Agatha M. Tiegel
Class of 1893
Presentation Day Exercises at
National Deaf-Mute College, April 26, 1893

Table of Contents

Foreword

This book is a heart-warming compilation of information, history, anecdotes, and research that showcases many, many deaf women from all walks of American life, past and present.

This book becomes a benchmark in the growing collection of literature developed by deaf authors and is a good companion to Jack Gannon's *Deaf Heritage* which did for the Deaf community what Arthur Haley's *Roots* did for the Black community—giving, for the first time, a sense of heritage, family bonds and pride.

"Deaf women?! What's there to say?" was the first thought that crossed my mind when I received my first request to speak on the subject of deaf women.

I felt that deafness was the larger and more complex issue that transcended other human characteristics such as gender, race, age. But being a good ol' Georgette who does it, I agreed to oblige with the request and spent time doing research and preparation. It turned out to be an enlightening experience for me.

First, I realized that being deaf and female was indeed a double-whammy! Both groups may suffer from stereotyped images, oppression by the majority, limited employment opportunities and lower pay. Being a deaf female could then result in second-class membership of either circle and thus a double dosage of negative ramifications. But, it doesn't have to! This is one important reason for the publication of this book.

Whether we know it or not, out thoughts, behavior, lifestyles and aspirations are influenced by individuals we admire, respect and look up to. If these individuals also share some of the same characteristics as we do—sex, handicap, race—their influence becomes stronger and emulating them becomes more of a reality, less of a fantasy. They become role models for us. They represent possibilities of what we, too, can become.

I have been asked who my role models were. My first role model was my mom, who, like me, is deaf. She's the best mom in the world . . . kind, smart, patient, beautiful and loving.

I remember vividly her coming to take me home from school on Fridays on the subway and how heads would turn! She was a fantastic cook, seamstress and story-teller. A model mom. That is still true, 40 years later.

Back in those days, my mom did not have any deaf teachers or administrators. When I was graduated from high school, I made a bee-line for "Happy Hunting Grounds" Gallaudet College to snare a husband, raise kids and live happily ever after, like my mom.

I majored in the Arts so that I could apply these skills to home-making. (Home Economics, Library Science and Education were also popular majors for women.) Fortunately for me, my husband Herb was more visionary and encouraged me to continue my education and start a career.

Deaf male leaders then became my new role models. Women tended to be cast in supporting roles, as wives, as was traditional and appropriate in the 1960s prior to the women's movement.

According to *Deaf Heritage* approximately 24 schools were founded by deaf men. Only one wife is given equal billing with her husband, whereas one can assume that most men were married and relying on their wives' support behind the scenes. Thus I learned that I had to search for deaf female leaders—and found them—in the nooks and crannies of our history. Deaf women can, and do, have many kinds of careers, interests, and skills!

This book identifies many different deaf women of early years and makes it so much easier to expose people to their many significant accomplishments. Readers now have access to a smorgasbord of deaf female role models and can choose whomever they want to emulate or surpass.

This book would not have happened without the work and love of its two authors, Sharon Wood on the Eastern Seaboard in Maryland, and Mabs Holcomb on the West Coast in California.

The twain did meet and inspire in many other women the sense of sharing experiences of trials and joys. Like a smorgasbord, while there's something for everyone, more items can be added as they become known or occured.

Roslyn Rosen, Ph.D., Dean
College for Continuing Education
Gallaudet University, Washington, D.C.

Introduction

The traditional role of deaf women through decades has been one of slow, significant social changes.

The first International Congress of Women (hearing) was held in London, England, in 1900. Deaf women then waited 76 years to have their first conference which took place in Washington, D.C., at Gallaudet College in 1976.

The result of the conference in 1976 was that many follow-up conferences for deaf women took place in various states. Workshops on relevant issues were offered by many local groups. The most popular topic has been *Assertiveness*.

The National Association of the Deaf (NAD) showed interest by appointing Gertrude Scott Galloway to chair the Women's Section in 1982; Vicky Hurwitz took over in 1984; Sharon Kay Wood is the current chairwoman, 1986–88.

Several research studies in the past few years have shown that deaf women seem to have low self-perceptions as individuals. Recently changing patterns have shown some progress in the life-styles of deaf women.

Yvonne Pitrois (1880–1937), a contributor to *The Silent Worker,* strongly believed that deaf children should learn their own special heritage.

In *Gallaudet Today,* spring 1974 special issue, Nancy Kelly Jones wrote "Where Are Our Deaf Women?." Ten years later, the summer 1984 issue followed with comments from the same woman explaining what had been happening in the past decade.

Deaf Women United was formed at the Deaf Women's Conference prior to the 1985 World Games of the Deaf in Los Angeles, California. The second conference was held in Washington, D.C., area during the summer of 1987.

There was a dearth of information about the role of women and minorities in the deaf world by Jack Gannon's book *Deaf Heritage, A Narrative History of Deaf in America.* Published in 1981, it contained few stories and names which aroused our curiosity about deaf women's roles in life. Harlan Lane's *When the Mind Hears* is another source of rich information on early education of the deaf.

This publication has been prepared with the sincere hope that it may serve to provide interesting material to those who wish to know and to honor the accomplishments of our deaf women.

We have aimed to bring out the high points of the careers of well-known deaf American women.

Professional magazines, newsletters and books on deaf people and deafness were used as primary sources of information. Personal interviews and correspondence with deaf women throughout America brought in boundless historic and fascinating facts.

The authors visited the Gallaudet University Archives, the San Francisco Public Library — Deaf Section, and the National Technical Institute for the Deaf (NTID) Resources Center at Rochester, New York, for additional guidance.

Deaf Women: A Parade Through the Decades attempts both to bring notable deaf women out of the mists of history into the spotlight, and to recognize our contemporaries.

Many pieces in this puzzle are missing. We hope that as you go through the tidbits contained in *Deaf Women* you will suddenly realize that you happen to possess a piece or two which will help complete this broad puzzle. We plan to include these and other pieces in a sequel.

Some day all these bits will go toward completing biographies of deaf women who have been of significance and impact. Their lives will provide role models for younger deaf women.

This explains why we decided to go ahead with this work, however incomplete. To wait until all pieces of the puzzle fit means to wait too long.

Early Years

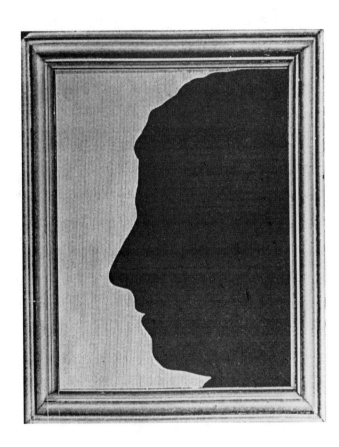

EARLY YEARS

It was two deaf sisters who influenced Abbe Charles Michel de l'Epee to become interested in educating deaf children. He founded the National Institution for the Deaf in Paris in the mid-18th Century. It was pure accident for him to become acquainted with those sisters when he visited their mother, as a priest (Bender 1970; 70–80).

It was a deaf girl whom Jacob Rodriques Pereira of Portugal fell in love with . . . and who inspired him to devote himself for years to the study of the education of the deaf in the mid-18th Century. But, another biographer mentioned that it was his own deaf sister who led him to become interested in teaching the deaf (Bender 1970; 73). Today, Jacob Rodriques Pereira is considered as the most honored educator of the deaf in Portugal.

Mary Bolling, (1766–1826) a descendant of John Smith and Indian Princess Pocahontas, was the first deaf American girl to receive a formal education. Born in Virginia, she and her two deaf brothers studied at the Braidwood School for the Deaf in Edinburgh, Scotland, between 1771 and 1783. The Braidwood family controlled deaf education in Britain from 1766 to 1825.

Later, Mary's father organized the first school for the deaf in America. It was known as "Cobbs," located in Virginia. The Braidwood Teaching Method was brought to this school. After eleven years it was closed due to inefficient management.

Thomas Hopkins Gallaudet, sponsored by Dr. Mason Fitch Cogswell and his friends, was sent to Europe, in 1815, to learn

methods of teaching the deaf. He brought back with him a bright, young, French, deaf teacher, Laurent Clerc. They co-founded the first permanent school for the deaf in America.

The Mary Augusta, the ship that brought them to the United States from France in 1816, was at sea for 52 days. During the lengthy voyage, Gallaudet tutored Clerc in English, and in return Clerc taught

Previous page. The only known portrait of Alice Cogswell, 1805–1831. Courtesy of Gallaudet Archives.

Thomas H. Gallaudet and Laurent Clerc co-founded Connecticut Asylum for the Education and Instruction of Deaf and Dumb Persons in Hartford, Ct. on April 15 with assistance of Alice Cogswell's father, Dr. Mason Cogswell. Alice was the first pupil of the first permanent school in 1817. Sophia Fowler was the 15th enrollee with her sister Parnel Flower a few months later. Elizabeth Boardman entered as the 17th pupil. Courtesy of Gallaudet Archives.

THE OLDEST SCHOOL FOR THE DEAF IN THE UNITED STATES

Founded 1817
Thomas H. Gallaudet, of Hartford, first Principal.
Laurent Clerc, of Paris, France, first Instructor.

THOMAS H. GALLAUDET   1817   1821   LAURENT CLERC

Copyright by C. E. Emery, 1916.

THE AMERICAN SCHOOL FOR THE DEAF, HARTFORD, CONN.

Gallaudet the sign language used in France.

The Connecticut Asylum for the Education and Instruction of the Deaf and Dumb, the first permanent school in America was opened with seven pupils on April 15, 1817, in Hartford, Connecticut. It is now known as the American School for the Deaf (ASD) in West Hartford.

Alice Cogswell (1805–1831), a neighbor and an inspiration to the Rev. Thomas Hopkins Gallaudet, attended a public school. There her teacher, Lydia Huntley Sigorney, communicated with her in home-made sign language.

It was for Alice that her father raised funds to send Thomas Hopkins Gallaudet to Europe to learn techniques of teaching the deaf. The formal education of the deaf in America originated from this point.

Alice completed her education in 1823. No one knows what she did after that until 1831 when her beloved father died in December. Her death came 13 days later, at the age of 25.

In his book, *Notable Deaf People*, G.C. Braddock wrote: *"Alice spelled out 'Cold, icy grave' and relapsed into a delirium in which she recognized none of her friends except one, Thomas Hopkins Gallaudet. He had come to pray for her in her last hours. She died peacefully, after watching his signs with interest."*

There is only one known portrait of Alice Cogswell. It was reproduced for the book *Biographical Sketch of Thomas Hopkins Gallaudet.*

"Grandma Gallaudet," circa 1865. Courtesy of Gallaudet Archives.

Thomas Hopkins Gallaudet, co-founder and Principal, married Sophia Fowler, not Alice Cogswell as is commonly thought.

Sophia Fowler (1798–1877) enrolled at the Asylum (ASD) at the age of 19 with her older sister and deaf cousin.

In 1821, after three years of education, her formal classes ended by a surprise marriage proposal by Thomas Hopkins Gallaudet. They had eight hearing children: four girls and four boys.

The Rev. Thomas Gallaudet, the eldest son, married a deaf woman, **Elizabeth Reynolds Budd** (1825–1903). They had a family of seven children and later had two deaf granddaughters, **Margaret Gillen Sherman** and **Eleanor Sherman Font**. He was the founder of

church missions to the deaf and of St. Ann's Church for the Deaf (Episcopal) in New York City.

The youngest son, **Edward Miner Gallaudet** (1837–1917), accepted a position at the new Columbia Institution for the Deaf and Dumb and Blind in Washington, D.C., in 1857. Amos Kendall advised that he bring his widowed mother with him. She was the first matron, including two years as head of the department that taught cooking, sewing and other household arts.

When Edward Miner Gallaudet came to Washington, D.C. from Hartford, Connecticut to become principal of the Columbia Institution, he brought with him a dream shared by his father, Thomas Hopkins Gallaudet, that this new school for deaf and blind children could grow to become a college for deaf students of the United States. In 1864, Gallaudet's dream became a reality when President Abraham Lincoln signed legislation enabling the Columbia Institution to grant college-level degrees.

Sophia Fowler is considered one of the first deaf lobbyists for deaf rights as she made many friends in Washington, D.C., including Congressmen. She was known as "Queen Sophia." In 1918 the first dormitory for women at Gallaudet was named Sophia Fowler Hall in dedication to her memory.

There is a monument bearing a tablet in memory of Sophia Fowler Gallaudet in Hartford, Connecticut. It was made possible by a fund collected by the deaf women of America and their friends.

Abigail Dillingham, aged 31, was one of the first seven pupils to be enrolled at the old ASD. She later became a teacher and it is believed that she was the first deaf female teacher of the deaf. She taught at the Pennsylvania Institution for the Deaf and Dumb founded in 1821 after studying for four years at the original ASD.

Abigail taught Wilson Winton, who was later recognized as the first American teacher of the deaf. He taught at ASD for 47 years. She had to leave the teaching profession in 1824 due to health problems.

Mary E. Rose Totten (1808–1897) was the youngest and smallest (nine years old) member of the first class at ASD in 1817. Her first marriage to a prominent hearing man — a member of New York society — was the talk of the town. She was one of the first deaf members of the faculty at Fanwood in 1822.

In the middle 1850's, Mary (who had been widowed) remarried and was considered one of the most-traveled deaf ladies in the nation. She became matron at schools for the deaf in North Carolina, Illinois, and New York, where her second husband taught.

Elizabeth Boardman Clerc and her daughter Eliza. Painting by Charles Wilson Peale.

Elizabeth Crocker Boardman (1792–1880) married Laurent Clerc, her first deaf teacher, in 1819. She could hear some and could speak well. They were happily married for more than 50 years. They married in spite of Thomas Hopkins Gallaudet's objection. Dr. Gallaudet was opposed to a deaf person marrying another deaf person because of his belief that their deafness would be inherited by their offspring. They had six hearing children. The Rev. Francis J. Clerc, a missionary to the deaf was the only one who pursued a career working with the deaf.

There is a painting of Mrs. Clerc by Charles Wilson Peale, teaching her daughter, Eliza, to fingerspell an "E." It is at ASD now after Superintendent E. Boatner recognized it in a civic leader's home in Connecticut. The donor, a Clerc descendant, agreed that it should be hung in the Superintendent's office at ASD.

There were many influential women in Laurent Clerc's life. Clerc named four of them for their significant roles in deaf history. They were Alice Cogswell, Julie Brace, who was deaf/blind, Elizabeth Boardman Clerc and Sophia Fowler Gallaudet.

Amos Kendall, a former Postmaster General under President Andrew Jackson, was dissatisfied with the education provided to deaf children in the District of Columbia. In 1856 he donated two-and-a-half acres for a school for the deaf, dumb, and blind.

Congress incorporated the Columbia Institution for the Deaf and Dumb and the Blind (1857) on Kendall's land. The school is now called Kendall Demonstration Elementary School and serves only the deaf. The blind children left in 1865 and the word "blind" was dropped from the school name. It used to be known as Kendall School until 1970 when Public Law 91-587 was passed by the Congress.

1857 Columbia Institution for the
     Deaf and Dumb and Blind
1864 Columbia Institution
1865 National Deaf-Mute College
1894 Gallaudet College
1986 Gallaudet University

Firsts

First Female Students at the National Deaf-Mute College

Nancy Carolyn Jones, a *hearing reference librarian* at Gallaudet, submitted her thesis, "Don't Take Any Aprons to College! A Study of the Beginning of Co-Education at Gallaudet College" to the Faculty of the Graduate School of the University of Maryland in partial fulfillment of the requirements for the degree of Master of Arts in 1983.

In her thesis, she stated that deaf women were offered higher education during 1864–70, but only six women took advantage of the opportunity. The doors were then officially closed to them until 1887.

Carolyn also wrote that these young women during the year 1864–70 did not advance beyond the first collegiate year; lack of scholarships and proper accommodations were probable reasons. The six women were: Emma Speak

Alto Lowman. Courtesy of Gallaudet Archives.

and Ann Szymaposkie (enrolled 1864–65); Ida Sartain and Adelaide Smith (1865-66); Lydia Kennedy (1865-67); and Lydia Mitchell (1868–70).

May Martin (1868–1908) was the first female college graduate to teach at her alma mater. After graduation in 1895, she accepted a teaching position at Columbia Institution for the Deaf and Dumb (Kendall School) which was also combined with an instructor's role at the college. She founded the "Buff and Blue" (student newspaper) in 1892 but let a male student be the editor-in-chief. Several years later she left her job to marry a Mr. Stafford and raise a family.

Alto Lowman was the first to graduate with a Bachelor of Philosophy degree in 1882. At her graduation, Dr. Edward Miner Gallaudet announced from the platform that all his doubts as to the advisability of admitting women were satisfied, and that henceforth their presence in the college would be an assured fact. She taught at both the North Dakota School for the Deaf in Devils Lake and the Maryland School for the Deaf in Frederick. One of the streets on Kendall Green (Gallaudet University campus) is named in her honor.

Kendall Green, ca 1867.
Courtesy of Gallaudet Archives.

Agatha Tiegel Hanson (1878–1959) of Pennsylvania was the first female to complete the full course at the National Deaf-Mute College. She was admitted in the year 1888 at the age of 15. She was the only female in her graduating class and was the Valedictorian.

Agatha married Olaf Hanson, a noted deaf architect who designed several schools for the deaf and public buildings in several cities. Before her marriage, she taught at the Minnesota School for the Deaf for six years.

Agatha Tiegel. Courtesy of Gallaudet Archives.

Bottom: First group of women joining Alto Lowman were Ella F. Black; Anna L. Kurtz from Indiana; Ellen Rudd of Nebraska; and Ida K. Kinney and Hattie A. Leffler of Pennsylvania–1887. Courtesy of Gallaudet Archives.

Agatha, one of the founding members of the O.W.L.S. (now Phi Kappa Zeta) was the first President of this sorority.

Agatha T. Hanson Plaza at Gallaudet University was named in her honor during the 1980s.

Quotes are excerpted from an article by Agatha in The National Exponent, March 28, 1985, *"And quite lately the additional information that an appropriate of $30,000 has been granted by Congress, and that at least part of it would be used in providing more commodious quarters for the young women, who are present uncomfortably crowded in the Kendall School building, makes it evident that the feminine portion of the student body is here to stay."*

Top: Colonel Bolling opened the short lived first school for the deaf in Cobbs, Virginia to public in 1815. In 1812, John Braidwood taught Mary Bolling and her brothers in a private class at Bolling Hall on campus. Illustration by one of the students at Cobbs.

Bottom: Sophia Fowler's last day at Gallaudet in Library of House One on Gallaudet Campus—1887. Courtesy of Gallaudet Archives.

Top: May Martin was the only female professor among the otherwise all-male faculty–1895. Courtesy of Gallaudet Archives.

Bottom: Clarke School in Northhampton, Mass., where Mabel Hubbard Bell attended. It was John Clarke, the banker and her father who founded the school–1867. Courtesy of Gallaudet Archives.

Top: Agatha Tiegel was the only female student in her senior class–1893. Courtesy of Gallaudet Archives.

Bottom: Maryland School in the city of Frederick (formerly called Fredericktown) where Alto Lowman completed high school– 1868. Courtesy of Gallaudet Archives.

Top: A male chaperone at Kentucky School for the Deaf with women students at a picnic–1916. Courtesy of Gallaudet Archives.

Bottom: Iowa School for the Deaf in Iowa City established in 1855; it became the second state residential school west of the Mississippi river before it was moved to Council Bluffs in the 1870's. Ethel Taylor Hall received her first schooling there. Courtesy of Gallaudet Archives.

DEAF WOMEN

Victorian Era

THE VICTORIAN ERA

Ethel Zoe Taylor Hall–on her graduation day–1900. Courtesy of Gallaudet Archives.

Ethel Taylor Hall (1878-1966) a native of Iowa was graduated from the Colorado School for the Deaf and from Gallaudet College. She married Percival Hall, a Professor of the college on her graduation day in 1900. He became the second President of Gallaudet College in 1910.

Ethel enjoyed the beauty of art; one of her paintings was exhibited at the St. Louis World's Fair in 1904.

By collecting old newspapers from door-to-door in the neighborhood, she raised scholarship funds for needy young female students at Gallaudet.

She was known for her love of gardening which beautified the Gallaudet campus during her days. Many old timers remember how she would call on male students to do the heavy work for her.

Previous page. The year of 1885. Courtesy of Gallaudet Archives.

The money they earned enabled them to afford to date the coeds.

Ethel bore three children; two sons, who were members of the Gallaudet faculty and a daughter. Percival Hall, Jr. had a home on Faculty Row. She lived on the campus for 64 years and in her latter years was known to collect dandelion greens and wild leeks on the lawns and on Hotchkiss Field.

The second wife, **Sarah Griswold** (1819–1901), of Samuel F. B. Morse, the famous inventor of the telegraph now used all over the world, was deaf. She was a product of the New York School for the Deaf (Fanwood).

Sarah supported her brother and his General Store with earnings from her sewing business before her marriage to Samuel Morse, her second cousin. It was she who inspired her husband to continue his project, a communication system — the telegraph using dots and dashes of the Morse Code. They communicated by using Morse Code on the hands.

A story in the *Rochester (N.Y.) Journal* in 1881 said, *"When Mr. Morse was trying to introduce his invention some years ago, Mr. Amos Kendall was one of his prospective backers. Kendall, a very wealthy and charitable man, became so interested in the deaf since meeting Mrs. Morse (Sarah Griswold Morse) that he determined to do all he could do to establish a school for deaf-mutes in Washington, D.C. He gave a large plot of ground toward it, now called Kendall Green, on which the buildings stand."*

Mr. Morse became Amos Kendall's financial manager; thus the first telegraph line ran through Kendall Green (Gallaudet University campus) from the Kendall home to Baltimore, on May 24, 1844.

Mabel Hubbard Bell (1858–1923) first knew Alexander Graham Bell, her future husband, at the School of Vocal Physiology for Teachers of the Deaf. He was teaching visible speech, a method invented by his father, Professor Alexander Melville Bell, for improving the articulation of the congenitally deaf students in Boston, Massachusetts. Mabel was one of the first pupils enrolled in the Clarke School at Northhampton, Massachusetts in 1867.

John Clarke, a local banker and philanthropist, donated $50,000 to establish this oral school.

Mabel helped a deaf oral man to establish the Nitchie School of lip-reading and the New York League for the Hard-of-Hearing to provide free lessons in lip-reading.

Mabel was a dramatic playwright and some of her works were published in more than 12 languages. She also founded *The Young Ladies' Club* which was the first women's club in Canada. For her outstanding work, she was named an honorary President.

"Mable Hubbard was young, lovely and RICH when Alexander Graham Bell, brilliant, ardent and POOR married her." — Reader's Digest, Feb. '87.

"One day, Mabel, an accomplished painter, told Bell she was receiving a painting. He was greatly surprised and amused

Mabel Hubbard and her husband Alexander Graham Bell. Reprint from The Silent Worker.

Juliette "Daisy" Gordon Low (1860–1927), a deafened (became deaf at a later age) woman, founded the Girl Scouts of U.S.A. in Savannah, Georgia, in 1912. She also started troops in England and Scotland before she returned to her home state, Georgia. She was buried in her Girl Scout Leader uniform.

The Illinois School for the Deaf, in 1919, was the first school to start a scout troop for deaf girls.

This founder of Girl Scouts of U.S.A. prided herself on her eccentricity and her stubbornness (which often got her into trouble) and used these qualities to show Victorian women that their lives could be whatever they dared to make them.

Juliette wanted young women to think big—to feel entitled to an education, career, and family if they wanted. Her conviction that girls should think of themselves as capable of becoming doctors, architects, or pilots, able to survive in the wild, and to know how to *"secure a burglar with eight inches of cord."* Her programs took thousands of girls out of their

when it turned out to be that of a sedate owl due, no doubt, to his habit of working on his inventions all night and sometimes well into the morning. The picture always hung over Dr. Bell's workbench.

"Mabel's deafness endeared her to her husband doubly, since his own mother had struggled with the same handicap from his ear-

liest recollections, and he always did his utmost to share remarks and news with her so that she would not feel isolated.

Vera S. Cassilly wrote in National Geographic Society, 1963, that Mrs. Bell's tact, generous understanding of her husband's temperamental needs, both for company and utter solitude, her common sense about business matters and her charm made her beloved wherever she went . . ."

Juliette "Daisy" Gordon Low.

homes to the outdoors and on to professional careers. She gave to many the beginnings of self-determination.

When she met Sir Robert Baden-Powell, founder of the Boy Scouts and Girl Guides, she became interested in the new youth movement. Thus, in 1912, Juliette gathered 18 girls to organize the first two American Girl Guide troops. Her niece was the first registered member.

At one time a doctor was consulted for an ear ache she was suffering, but instead of letting him treat her according to conventional medical knowledge, she insisted that he use silver nitrate because she had heard about it as a new treatment.

Tragically, the potent solution rendered her partially deaf in one ear for life. In a freak accident at her wedding, a grain of rice lodged in her other ear. After its removal she was completely deaf in that ear.

Nancy Lyon, in her 1981 biography, *Lost Women: Juliette Low — The Eccentric Who Founded the Girl Scouts,* wrote that Juliette once called upon a woman she hardly knew to take charge of a project. The woman, certain she did not have the qualifications for the job, declined it. Low, using her deafness to pretend not to hear the woman's refusals, said cheerfully, *"Then that's settled. I have told my girls you will take the meeting next Thursday."* The woman took the job without another word.

Arthur Gordon wrote in his article *"I Remember Aunt Daisy": "Although her deafness was a constant trial for her, Daisy (Juliette Gordon Low) could always joke about it. Once, listening to a*

speech of which she could not hear a word, she decided the speaker wasn't getting enough encouragement. So she applauded loud and long, and only discovered later that what she was cheering was a glowing eulogy of herself."

The World War II Liberty ship named for Juliette "Daisy" Gordon Low had the traditional champagne christening and launching rites in Georgia. It was a vessel used to bring American troops and supplies overseas.

Ida Montgomery, ca 1920. Courtesy of Gallaudet Archives.

Ida Montgomery (1840–1924), a teacher at the New York Institution for the Deaf (Fanwood) for 40 years, had taught all grade levels in the school.

She spent every summer at her summer cottage which overlooked a rocky beach at Nantucket, Massachusetts. Her place on the cliff with a hedge of Rosa Rugosa and her glorious crimson rambler roses was a showplace. All sight-seeing parties were brought to admire the spectacle.

The Prince of Wales changed the route of his historic tour of the United States to visit Ida's class and took over teaching for a while in her classroom. His wife, Princess Alexandria, had a hearing problem.

During Ida's retirement years, she shared living quarters with Elizabeth Peet in Washington, D.C. and taught the co-eds of Gallaudet the beauty of sign language. She, herself, excelled in grace and forcefulness, memorizing and silently signing the songs of the era.

Elizabeth Peet (1874–1962), the former Gallaudet Professor and Dean of Women, was a daughter of deaf poetess **Mary Toles Peet** and a descendant of a family famed for its education of the deaf at New York's Fanwood (a residence hall there is named for the Peet family). She became deaf at a late age and wore a hearing aid.

Miss Peet was famed for being very prim and proper. She used to say during her Gallaudet years (1910–1951) that "holding hands leads to babies" and kissing would get one thrown out of college.

One day she noticed a young fellow sticking up his middle finger at her. She did not know what it meant so she asked him to explain. Nearly paralyzed with fright, the only thing he could think of at the moment was, *"It's a new popular sign for 'Good Morning'."* She believed him until someone finally had the courage to tell her the truth.

A few days later in a class with this same boy in it, she entered the room saying, "Good morning" the

DEAF WOMEN

proper way to all students until she approached that boy. She used her middle finger to him.

Miss Peet refused to allow the boys and girls to swim together in the same pool. She would let the boys swim first and then have it drained and refilled for the girls. It was said that she feared the girls would become pregnant if they swam in the water after the boys polluted it.

"Peetums," as she was popularly known during World War II years died unmarried at the age of 87. Charles Ely, a dashing bachelor Professor at Gallaudet during her salad days, smoked cigars. They dated and one day Miss Peet told Professor Ely to choose between her and his cigars. You can guess his choice.

Clara Belle Rogers, over 40-year instructor at South Carolina School for the Deaf, wrote in 1946, "My sister Antoinette Sarah (Rogers) of class '99 helped President E. M. Gallaudet in getting money from Congress for the college by talking to them for Dr. Gallaudet. She was his favorite.

After leaving Gallaudet, several of the women became leaders in the world. These schoolings had expanded their horizons and they, in turn, had enriched the college and the society of deaf and hearing.

Left: Elizabeth Peet. Courtesy of Gallaudet Archives.

Bottom: Classroom at Western Pennsylvania School of the Deaf–1910. Courtesy of Gallaudet Archives.

DEAF WOMEN

Opposite, top: Increased enrollment of women at Gallaudet College during the early 1900's. Courtesy of Gallaudet Archives.

Opposite, bottom: Picture taken during their introductory year, the first year renaming National College Deaf-Mute to Gallaudet College—1894. Courtesy of Gallaudet Archives.

Top: A holiday tea party. The college has grown and continues to grow, ca 1905. Courtesy of Gallaudet Archives.

Left: Jeanie Lippet's father, the governor of Rhode Island, found out his 4-year old Jeanie (1870–1940) became deaf from scarlet fever. In 1877, Jeanie was invited to speak (use oral method) in favor of the bill to construct a school for the deaf. She was appointed to the board till 1906. Reprint from Volta Review.

Top: Class of 1903 graduation picture.
Courtesy of Gallaudet Archives.

Bottom: The new prep coeds line up in front of
Fowler Hall, so the Upper Classmen can tease
them—1939. Courtesy of Eric Malzkhun.

Art

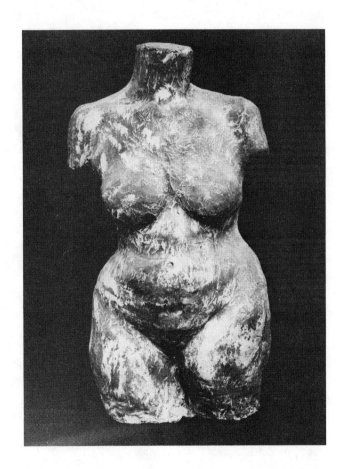

Daniel Chester French's one-and-a-half-ton statue of Thomas Hopkins Gallaudet and Alice Cogswell stands in the front of Chapel Hall on the Gallaudet University campus. The statue was commissioned by the National Association of the Deaf (NAD) in 1887 and individual deaf people, women's clubs, many deaf organizations and friends contributed to its funding.

Thomas Hopkins and Alice temporarily left their home on Kendall Green in 1976–77 to visit museums in New York City, Washington, Detroit, and Boston. There is a smaller replica of the statue at the American School for the Deaf in Hartford, Connecticut.

Legend has it that a friend of French's advised him that Gallaudet's legs were too short. The sculptor postponed his wedding in order to extend the legs an inch or two.

The American Society of Deaf Artists was founded in 1907. Miss Abrams was the only woman who ever served as President of this Society. She was honored at a 20th anniversary banquet at Brooklyn, New York in 1926.

Margaret E. Jackson (1902–1986) was known worldwide for her work as the Curator of Photography for the American Hispanic Society of New York City. She was recognized as one of the leading authorities in micro- and macro-photography by many museums.

"Despite all of the serious and delicate work she has done," stated the Jersey School News in September 1985, *"Miss Margaret*

Previous page. Sculpture by Yola Rozynek.

Alice Cogswell & Thomas Hopkins Gallaudet Statue, ca. 1920. Courtesy of Lois Hoover.

Jackson liked to recall the humorous things that have happened to her."

On one occasion, Margaret was sent to Spain and Portugal on a photographic assignment by the museum. Each night she would develop her pictures in the bathroom of her hotel room. Then, with many feet of string, she would hang her film all over the room so it would dry. This worked fine until one morning, while her breakfast was being delivered, the door was opened, breaking the string. Down

came the whole mess and Margaret ended up looking like a well-decorated Christmas tree.

Poetess Alice McVan was known and respected for her work translating Spanish lyrics. They appeared in publications of the Hispanic Society in New York City. Tryst is considered her best and most impressive work.

After graduation from Gallaudet College in 1921, Florence Louis May started her professional

Alice McVan

This was mainly accomplished by sales of the Thomas Gallaudet (1822–1902) stamp.

A painting (circa 1600) showing French educator Pereir teaching very young, deaf Marie Magdeline Marios speech in the Museum of the Deaf in Paris.

Only two female artists were recognized in the 1981 book by Gannon; **Regina Hughes**, a scientific illustrator, and **Dr. Betty Miller**, an artist satirizing manualism versus oralism.

In 1967, Gallaudet College bestowed upon **Regina Olson Hughes**, 1918 Gallaudet graduate, the honorary degree of Doctor of Humane Letters. This was in recognition of her outstanding work as a scientific illustrator in botany. She had been drawing for the Agricultural Research Service of the U.S. Department of Agriculture since 1936. There is also a plant named in her honor — Billbergia Regina. She continues to work as a volunteer illustrator.

Regina Olson Hughes. Photo Credit: Charles Shoup, Gallaudet.

career at the Hispanic Society of America, New York City, as an assistant in the museum department.

She advanced from Museum Cataloguer to Assistant Curator to Curator of Textiles.

Florence toured the great museums of Spain and traveled throughout the United States to visit museums and authorities on Spanish culture.

Gallaudet College granted her an honorary M.A. degree in 1945.

Florence Louis May, Alice Jan McVan and Margaret E. Jackson were pioneers for their work in illustrations of Spanish relics. These were published by the Hispanic Society of America, New York, during the late 1920s and early 1930s.

Eleanor Sherman Font, great-granddaughter of Thomas Hopkins and Sophia Fowler Gallaudet, was the chairwoman of the International Exhibitions of Fine and Applied Arts by Deaf Artists in New York City in 1933-34. She was instrumental in establishing the Gallaudet Home Society, Inc. to raise funds for the Gallaudet Home for Aged and Infirm Deaf in Poughkeepsie, New York.

Betty G. Miller

Betty G. Miller is a well-known professional artist who taught art at Gallaudet College for 18 years. She was the first deaf woman to receive her doctorate degree from Pennsylvania State University in 1976. During 1977, in Austin, Texas, she co-founded Spectrum, Focus on Deaf Artists.

Betty has participated in many art shows, primarily in Washington, D.C., Texas and northern California. She is known for her visual representation of her Deaf Experience, some of which has been published in *Deaf Heritage* by Jack Gannon. Currently, she is leading a double life in the Washington area as both professional artist and as a consultant and counselor in the area of alcohol and drug abuse with Deafpride, Inc.

Jean Pearl Chan, a native of Hong Kong, was encouraged to draw while very young. Later, she took art classes at the Chinese University in Hong Kong. She moved to Portland, Oregon with her family and has her own studio in her home where she specializes in Chinese paintings.

"Since I lost my hearing when I was three years old," says Jane Pearl Chan, *"it is difficult for me to remember how to speak. I feel that my paintings speak for my heart, and for my love in the beauty of Chinese art."*

Linda Tom, an illustrator at the Washington, D.C. Navy Yard, is also a free lancer with a studio of her own. She was graduated from the California School for the Deaf, Berkeley, in 1966.

Jodi Blank, of Los Angeles, was the first person to introduce and incorporate an Arts Festival into the World Games of the Deaf, Summer 1985. WGD never had an arts festival before.

Myung Jo Sweeney, a teenager, won first place in painting for her age level at the 11th Annual International Creative Arts Festival at Des Plaines, Illinois, in 1987. My Jo, a talented artist, had been in the art program for three years at the California School for the Deaf (now in Fremont).

Eulalia Stakley Burdick, of Akron, Ohio, had a collection of over 10,000 old buttons. She won

Eulalia Stakley Burdick's buttons.

several blue ribbons for her displays. Her favorites were those from military uniforms with the manual alphabet letters worn by cadets at the New York School for the Deaf (Fanwood).

Many of her buttons depicted characters from Aesop's Fables; others were copies of cameos of noted women of the 19th Century.

"Coffin Door" (Chapel Hall at Gallaudet) illustrated by Ruth Peterson.

Ruth Ricker Peterson, of Rochester, New York, is known for her expertise in sketching. Many pieces of her work in a variety of books and exhibits in the D.C. area received recognition as well as awards. She contributed several humorous sketches and a beautiful one of the *Coffin Door* at Gallaudet University to this book.

Ann Silver of New York City designed and illustrated over 20 sign language textbooks, dictionaries and children's books and developed many sign language/deafness logos.

Ann Silver. Photo Credit: Gallaudet Photo Lab.

While working for the signed English Project at Gallaudet, she illustrated 14 books in a series for children. As a freelance illustrator she did *Sign Talk* an international hand alphabet and contributed to Sternberg's *American Sign Language—A Comprehensive Dictionary.*

The 11th Annual Outstanding Young Alumnus Award, sponsored by the GUAA, went to Ann Silver. This honor goes to an alumnus who "in the past 15 years has performed some impressive service to the University and/or the deaf community or who has brought favorable recognition to our alma mater through some notable achievement in his or her personal or professional life." She was from Washington State.

Ann has achieved prominence as an art illustrator, a communicator and an advocate. She is an activist in the field of cultural arts within the deaf community and has served on the Boards of Directors of the American Arts of the Deaf, Deaf Artists of America, and as the deaf representative on the National Endowment for the Arts Museum Task Force. She has designed and illustrated over 20 sign language textbooks, dictionaries and children's books.

A regular columnist on Deaf Culture for *The Silent News,* Ann was often brought in as a consultant to New York's Metropolitan Museum of Art to prepare proper, accessible programs for deaf visitors.

She has a collection of over 800 hands of all sizes, shapes and textures and has been doing research for a book on the ILY (I Love You) sign.

Ellen Roth, a New York artist who earned a B.F.A. degree from New York University, presented a slide show, *Women's Murals* at the second Deaf Women Conference at George Mason University, Fairfax, Virginia, in the summer of 1987.

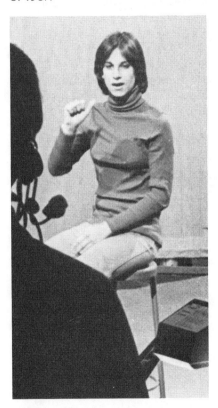

Ellen Roth. Photo Credit: Gallaudet Photo Lab.

Photography

Dorothy "Dody" Ellis, an IBM computer programmer in San Jose, California, is a free-lance photographer. All her life she has enjoyed taking candid pictures reflecting the characters of people in many walks of life.

Recently, Dody has started three private collections: Notable Deaf Activists; Children in Classrooms at the California School for the Deaf/Fremont; and Face Mask Entertainment. The collections were on exhibit at the 1987 California Association of the Deaf Convention in Santa Clara.

"I've always believed in destiny," says Dody, repeating a favorite quotation. *"What's life? What's the purpose? In order to fulfill my destiny, I believe in Imagination, Visualization, Concentration and Realization (ICVR).*

"After the realization," Dody continued, *"it leaves one a feeling of satisfaction in fulfilling the purpose of life. It also gives an inspiration to other lives. We, who create such an inspiration, are contributing members of our world."*

Maggie Lee Sayer, deaf, was born to houseboaters in 1920 on the riverbanks of Paducah, Kentucky. When her older sister **Myrtle** and Maggie reached school age, they attended Kentucky School for the Deaf and stayed at school for nine months out of the academic year, and then spent the summers on their fifty-foot floating home that their father built on the Tennes-

Maggie Lee Sayer. Photo Credit: Gallaudet Photo Lab.

see River. By 1971, after a half century of riverboat life, she moved her home to land where she is now at a nursing home in Parsons. She is part of Tennessee River History.

While still in her teens, using a Kodak box camera, Maggie began recording her life on film. Her photographs show a long-gone river culture that included her family, friends in a lifestyle of meager subsistence.

The camera gave Maggie the means to broaden her methods of communication with visual expression. Her pictures are of considerable value to historians attempting to document what had once been a thriving, if impoverished, community of river dwellers.

Deaf Artists of America (DAA), formed in 1985 published its first quarterly newsletter in January, 1986. Its initial national artists con-

ference was held at NTID in Rochester, New York, in 1987.

Featured were workshops conducted by **Elaine Montoya**, of Albuquerque, New Mexico; **Robin Bartholick**, of Seattle, Washington; **Doris Jean Cox** of Tennessee, a renowned researcher of ancient weaving techniques; and **Joan Popovich Kitscher** of California, artist and story-telling performer.

There were other workshops sponsored by the National Theatre of the Deaf with **Sandi Inches-Vasnick** and others. **Debbie Rennie**, woman of 1000 faces, performed Creative Expressions in Sign Language.

Commemorative Postage Stamps

Juliette Gordon Low, founder of the Girl Scouts, was honored with a three-cent commemorative stamp. The green, first-class postage stamp was first placed on sale on Oct. 29, 1948, at Savannah, Georgia, the birthplace of Juliette.

Helen Keller was also recognized for her endeavors as a deaf-blind humanitarian. The 15-cent commemorative, marking the centennial of her birth, was first issued on June 27, 1980, in her home town of Tuscumbia, Ala.

These were the only two deaf women honored by the United States Postal Service.

Deborah "Debbie" M. Sonnenstrahl of Washington, D.C., is Associate Professor of Art History and Museum Studies at Gallaudet University. Debbie was the first deaf person awarded a Master's degree in Art History from Catholic University of America, in 1976, and then went on to become the first deaf person to be awarded a Ph.D. Degree in Museum Studies and Deaf Education from New York University.

Debbie, who has been listed in *Who's Who In America,* has been honored with many awards;

"Debbie" Sonenstrahl

including Teacher of the Year, Best Actress Awards, and honors in Community Services.

The Docents for the Deaf at M.H. DeYoung Museum, Golden Gate Park, San Francisco, and the Oakland Museum, have been offering monthly signed tours since 1977. The docents take sign language courses, learning specific signs for deaf museum visitors. Joyce McCallon Lynch,

Joanne Kovach Jauregui and Marilyn Duncan McCallon were among the tutors.

Mildred Albronda, the deafened author of *Douglas Tilden, Portrait of a Deaf Sculptor,* wrote that the model for his famed Admission Day statue was his deaf wife. The sculpture stands at the world-famed intersection of Market, Post and Montgomery Streets in San Francisco, California.

Rosalyn Lee Gannon, a graduate of the North Carolina School and an art major at Gallaudet has won

Rosalyn Lee Gannon. Gallaudet Photo Lab.

recognition for her work as a pointillist.

In the Latham Foundation International Humane Poster Contest, Art Schools and Universities category, she won honors in the 1959 Prize Awards. Her work, a still life, also won honorable mention in the Hughes Contest at Gallaudet.

She designed the cover of *Deaf Heritage* written by her husband, Jack Gannon.

3¢ 3¢
FOUNDER OF THE GIRL SCOUTS OF THE U.S.A.
JULIETTE GORDON LOW
UNITED STATES POSTAGE

Linda Tom & LCTOM Studio booth. Photo
Credit: Gallaudet Photo Lab.

Black Deaf

BLACK DEAF

Amanda A. Johnson, a graduate of the North Carolina Institution for Colored Deaf and Dumb and Blind in Raleigh, was the first black female teacher. Amanda was one of the large number of the graduates from this institute that taught in many parts of the nation where black children were educated in segregated schools. She taught at the Texas Institute for the Deaf, Dumb, and Blind Colored Young on a farm near Austin, Texas, circa 1887.

William C. Ritter, of Virginia, was concerned that colored deaf children knew nothing about salvation. Many of them didn't know their own names. Through his efforts, the Virginia School for Colored Deaf and Blind Children was opened in Hampton in 1909. His deaf wife from North Carolina, was the first teacher.

"To do missionary work among the colored is not to do a favor to them," wrote **Blanche W. Williams** in a 1927 issue of *The Silent Worker. "They have a right to an equal chance with the white man, an equal chance in education to encourage self-improvement and to create high ideals of conduct.*

"They need white friends, but by taking charge of ministering to their mission only weakens them in self-reliance. Our best friends," she concluded, *"are those who help us to help ourselves. This field of work is unlimited."*

Frances M. McAndrew (Caucasian) taught at several schools, but she was best known for her contribution to the School for the Colored Deaf at Overlea, Mary-

Previous page. Virginia School at Hampton, women signing "Nearer My God to Thee"– 1948. Courtesy of Gallaudet Archives.

land, in the 1920's and 1930's.

James Gilbert, Jr. of Cincinnati, Ohio, was the first and only colored student to be admitted to The National Deaf-Mute College before 1950. He was a graduate of the Ohio School for the Deaf in 1880. In 1950, when the student body itself that paved the way for black people to be admitted by sending its wrestlers against Howard University's team a year ago, it made the decision of the College authorities easier to open the door for the blacks.

Ida Gray Hampton, on the panel at the Centennial Program at Gallaudet in October, 1987. Gallaudet Photo Lab.

In 1957 Ida Wynette Gray Hampton was the first black deaf woman to be graduated from Gallaudet College. She has been teaching at the Florida School for the Deaf in St. Augustine, since 1957. She was on the panel at the Centennial Program at Gallaudet in October, 1987.

Until the early 1960's, schools began to integrate black students into the mainstream by law. **Lottie Mae Crook** was one of the first blacks to enter a white school for the deaf. Deaf from the age of ten, she is a 1957 graduate of the Alabama School for Negro Deaf in Talladega.

She then lost her black friends when she went to a white school; the whites did not accept her; and her deafness was another handicap. She was in limbo, but more for her color than for her deafness. She continued on to Gallaudet where the social reception was better. She received her Bachelor of Arts Degree in English from Gallaudet on June 4, 1962.

Lottie, one of the founders and a Past President of the Black Deaf Advocates, works in the U.S. Treasury in Washington, D.C.

Black Deaf Advocates was established in 1981. The first national BDA Conference was held in Cleveland, Ohio in 1982. **Sherry Emery** of Kansas City, Missouri was the first President of the BDA.

Other active members of Black Deaf Advocates are **Jeannette Stone** and **Shirlene Williams**, both of Chicago.

Elizabeth Moore Aviles, a graduate of the Pennsylvania School for the Deaf and of Gallaudet, is now a Project A.I.D.S. specialist at Deafpride, Inc. in Washington, D.C.

All these black deaf activists were facilitators at the Second Deaf Women United (DWU) Conference in 1987.

"I went to the Maryland School for the Colored Blind and Deaf in Overlea, near Baltimore," said **Helen Johnson Luckey**. "I had white teachers who encouraged me to go to college. I did not realize that in those days Gallaudet College did not admit black students.

"I was disappointed as I knew I would not be happy in a public college for colored students. I asked my principal to let me return to school for some postgraduate work; at the time, 1942, I was 16 years old.

"During those extra years," Helen continued, "I learned a lot from those deaf teachers fresh from Gallaudet College."

Nathie Lee Marbury, a Western Pennsylvania School for the Deaf graduate, was the first black deaf woman to enter the National Leadership Training Program at CSUN in January 1987. She was also the first black, deaf, female instructor to be employed at KDES in Washington, D.C., where she was a communication specialist in sign language. She is renowned for signing recitation of "The Impossible Dream" and the National Anthem. She served the school from 1978 to 1986.

Michelle Banks received a prize for her performances in the roles of Titania (Shakespeare's play *A Midsummer Night's Dream*) and *Miss Brown* (in the Broadway

Nathie Lee Marbury

show, *For Colored Girls*).

Sheryl Guest Emery, 1982 Gallaudet graduate, a social worker with the Deaf, Hearing and Speech Center, in Detroit, Michigan, did two internships on Capital Hill during her Gallaudet days. She worked with Congressman Fred Richmond of New York, and then with Senator Robert Dole of Kansas, her home state.

"I am now serving as director of the National Black Advocates," Sheryl stated. "It is a fairly new organization, and I am happy to see it continue to grow.

"I am still active politically," Sheryl added. "Recently I was chosen for governor's appointment to the State Mental Health Council for the State of Michigan."

Tejese Wright —"Celebration of Citizenship" on Capitol Hill, Washington, D.C. Gallaudet Photo Lab.

Carolyn McCaskill Emerson

Carolyn McCaskill Emerson, of Alabama, who in 1980 was the first black girl elected Miss Gallaudet, is now a counselor for the deaf at Houston (Texas) Community College. She earned her B.A. in Psychology/Social Work and an M.A. in rehabilitation counseling.

Carolyn was presented the *"Employee-of-the-Year"* Award at Houston Community College in 1987. The prizes were cash donated in her name to a scholarship fund and a reserved parking space on the campus for one year. In 1986 and 1988, she coordinated the Deaf Women Texans' Conference held at the college.

Debbie Sonnestrahl (Caucasian) was the first notable deaf female director of plays for the deaf. She directed the first all-black cast play at a Black Deaf Advocates convention.

Shirley Allen, formerly with Gallaudet, now with NTID, had the leading role in that play. Shirley earned an M.A. in Guidance and Counseling from Howard University in 1972. *"Teaching to 'think positive',"* she commented, *"is the hardest job around today."*

Shirley Allen

At Sisterfire Festival in Washington, D.C., and at the second DWU conference at Fairfax, Virginia, the summer of 1987, Carrie Alexander (59 years old) and Goldie Thomas (87 years old) were introduced to the audience by Jan DeLap to share their experiences of racial discrimination during their childhood and adult years.

Mary Lynch Van Manen was the first black woman to compete in the World Games for the Deaf. She was a Gallaudet student when she competed in Helsinki, Finland, in 1961, taking ninth place in the running broad jump. Mary was also a member of the U.S. 4x100-meter relay team.

Diane Brooks at N.T.I.D. assumed the management position of Career Outreach and Enrollment Services in 1987. She was a transfer from Career Opportunities Office where she had been employed for several years. She was the first Black faculty member at Gallaudet.

Katie Brown, a retired counselor at the Jewish Vocational Service Agency in Chicago, has served on both the National Advisory Group (NAG) of N.T.I.D. and the Gallaudet College Board of Trustees; the first Black deaf woman to serve and she resigned after ten years.

Katie was very active in college campus events during her years there, winning many awards and scholarships. The prize monies helped pay her way through Gallaudet, where she earned both Bachelor's and Master's degrees.

Katie Brown

Before surgery for cataracts, **Mary Cheese** was blind for a year when she was very young. At the age of 13, she became deaf due to illness. Additional health problems prevented her from getting a college education. It did not stop her from being known as "Mother Superior" by many black deaf youngsters and adults in New York City today.

Azie Taylor Morton, Treasurer of the United States under President James Carter (1980), had deaf parents. Azie's name appeared on our currency during her term in office.

As a part of *A Celebration of Citizenship* program on nationwide television on September 17, 1987, President Ronald Reagan was joined by two students from K.D.E.S., **Tyese Wright**, 7, and a schoolmate, leading the nation's students in the Pledge of Allegiance to the Flag in American Sign Language.

Ruth Reed is a native of Chicago. In 1974, she was the first black woman from Illinois School for the Deaf to enroll Gallaudet College. After six years as a resident assistant at MSSD, she joined the KDES staff. She travels and performs with **Angela McCaskill-Gilchrist** and **Evon Black**, dancing and signing songs.

Lois Dadzie is an advocate for the Black deaf in the San Francisco Bay Area. Her husband is from Africa and they dedicate their lives to help their people here. **Beverly Knight** is another Californian working for the same cause.

Point of View
— Evelyn Lipshutz Zola

In 1970 I was a participant in a 1-month session of the DAWN program — Deaf Adults With Needs. This sequential program was continuing education related to Adult Basic Education.

I was in my forties at the time. I lived in Milwaukee (Wisc.) but the workshop was being held in Pittsburgh. The participants came from various areas east of the Mississippi River. After the first week of classes, the others all decided to go out of town for the weekend. That left the black instructor, B.J. and me in the dorms.

On the first Saturday, B.J. got the idea to take me out for the day. I thought to myself, *"Oh, a white married woman with a black, divorced man going out on a date."* I felt I had no choice but to go along. After the film we headed for the dorms. I said, *"Good night."* He had been a perfect gentleman.

Six months later we had a follow-up meeting. I saw B.J. again. We were both happy to see each other again. We started chatting about our past experiences. I was surprised to discover that our day together was the first experience B.J. had ever had with a deaf person. He told me what a thrill it was for him to interact — and to spend time — with a deaf person.

All along I had been concerned about black vs. white, while B.J. had been focusing on deaf vs. hearing. It all depends on your point of view.

Ruth Reed

Top: Black children posed with students of Columbia Institution for the Instruction of the Deaf and Dumb before sending to Maryland School for the Colored Blind and Deaf in Over-lea, Maryland, ca 1871. Courtesy of Gallaudet Archives.

Bottom: A segregated class at Kendall School, ca 1950's.

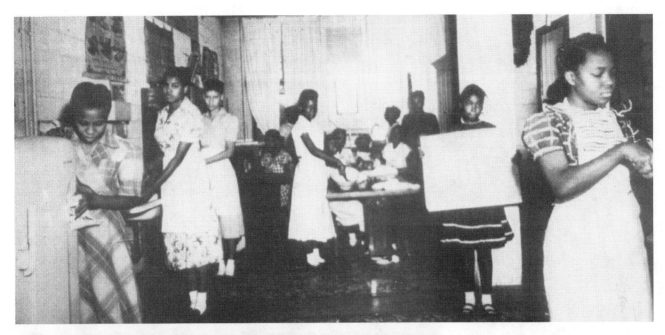

Top: Tennessee School for the Colored Deaf & Dumb Children in East Knoxville (1881). Courtesy of Gallaudet Archives.

Bottom: Michelle Banks.

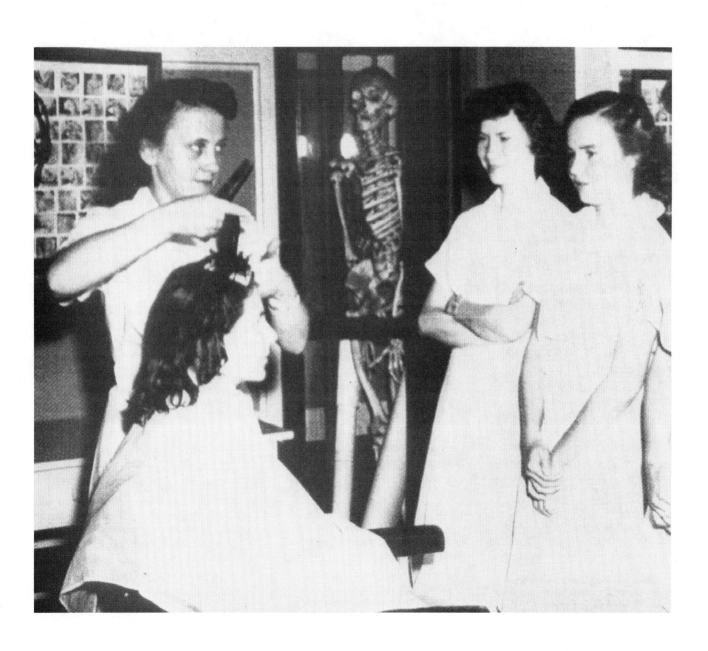

BUSINESS WORLD

Several studies on occupational conditions among deaf people show that those who have minimal communication skills tend to gravitate to more menial jobs.

In the Department of Labor Dictionary of Occupational Titles published in 1965, only 805 jobs were identified as suitable for deaf people. There is now a broad coalition of deaf organizations pressing for economic improvement.

Women, many of them deaf, are now moving into traditionally male-dominated fields.

Ann Szymaposkie was the first deaf person to work in a federal agency in Washington, D.C. Amos Kendall was the key man who made it possible.

A graduate of the Columbia Institution (Kendall School) in 1864, and with only a year at the National Deaf-Mute College, Ann was hired at the U.S. Treasury Department. She left college due to financial hardship.

Ollie Smoak Lynn was the U.S. Postmistress of Filbert, South Carolina, for over 20 years. In 1907 she won the competitive Civil Service Service examination, over four men, and conducted the business by the use of pad and pencil.

Girls at the Ohio School, during the late 1920's, were encouraged to take up printing because the superintendent knew they could make more money than by working in an office typing and filing.

Mabel Luddy had a coveted position as a clerk in the County Court House in Oakland, California, in the 1920s. She was well-

Previous page. Young women were being trained into cosmetology—1950. Courtesy of Gallaudet Archives.

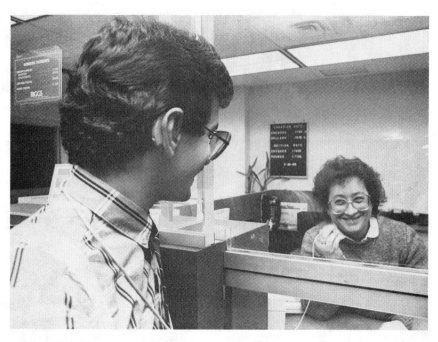

Diane Solomon Lockhart, bankteller. Gallaudet Photo Lab.

paid and the hours were short.

During the depression years, many deaf women kept their marriages secret as they wished to go on working. They needed money to build their funds for "dream" homes.

In Spartanburg, South Carolina, Mary Jane McCrorey, wife of a teacher at the South Carolina School and mother of five children was a hotel proprietress during the 1920's.

There were many deaf women who ran businesses in the 1920's –1930's, i.e., Harriet Hall, a millinery shop at Benton, Arkansas; Eva Maude Caldwell Hainline, a leading photography studio at Elkhart, Indiana; Emma Macy King, owned an orange grove in California.

Gerri Ehrlich, a Blackjack dealer at the Flamingo Hilton in Las Vegas, also conducts classes on rules and principles for playing casino games. She is also a travel consultant.

Ruth Yoder Skinner, co-foun-

der of the Southern California Women's Club of the Deaf is also the director of Interpre-Tours. Under her guidance, travel becomes a happy experience, not just a trip.

The travel business taught Ruth not only to help travelers but also how to meet and be comfortable with strangers and how to deal with people of many nationalities and races.

"When my group was in China, we visited a school for the deaf," relates Ruth. *"We collected cash donations as a gift for the school officials.*

"To my surprise, the gift was politely refused because the Chinese government forbids cash gifts, but anything other than money would be acceptable.

"A couple of Chinese teachers took us across the street to a school supply store," continued Ruth.

"We ordered supplies of paper, pencils, pens, rulers, books, and some electronic calculators. We kept on buying the stuff until we ran out of cash. To our surprise, big crowds of curious Chinese people had gathered in the store to watch us."

Hester Gregory started a boarding house in California in the 1920s so that deaf adults could live together rather than living separately all over town. She named it Rest Haven and only deaf boarders were allowed to board there. Miss Gregory soon found three deaf women to help her with housework. Over a period of time she had 85 men and women boarders.

Lori Kronick Bonheyo, former Talkin' Hands performer of the Washington, D.C. metro area, is now the first deaf co-owner of T.H. Wave, a Dee Jay business. T.H. Wave provides the hottest music with captioned videos. They play New Wave, Rock N' Roll and soul music at banquets, weddings, private parties and special events.

"It's a business that makes deaf people feel part of the music world and for hearing people to be part of us," quotes Lori.

Software 'N' Things, in Maryland, is owned by **Myrna Orleck-Aiello**. Her store offers service and selection of computers, softwares and accessories.

"It is unusual for a woman to own a business," writes Myrna, *"and even more so for someone who is hearing-impaired. My hearing loss doesn't stop me from providing quality service to customers."*

Reatha Suttka founded the French Reweaving Co. in Cincinnati, and employed many deaf women. Later in the '50s, she branched out to Chicago and other cities.

Sara Henson Peltier is the deaf owner-manager of the Mountain Springs Cottages in Chandler, North Carolina, which is close to the foot of Mt. Pisgah and the Blue Ridge Mountains.

Virginia "Ginny" Hartling of Massachusetts decided to take over her husband's six-year-old communications business after he passed away in 1987. Now her goal is to install TDDs at police stations, fire departments, airports and pharmacies.

In Rockville, Maryland, **Dot Brenner**, president of Potomac Telecom, Inc., deals with sales, services and supplies for telecommunication devices.

Nelda Rainey of Watsonville, California, grew up hard-of-hearing and lost most of the rest of her hearing when she was in her thirties.

Her education was in mechanical drawing and she worked in the microwave devices division of Sylvania/Litton Industries.

After five years with Sylvania/Litton, she transferred to Chemcut Corporation, the company that pioneered the chemical etching process used today to make printed circuit boards.

Eventually she made the transition from drafting to office management with new car dealerships.

"Sometimes I am not sure how much of my success is due to Karma," she remarked, *"but I wish everyone could be as lucky as I have been."*

Corinne E. Brannan Dori has been the Assistant Director of Financial Aid at the University of Massachusetts at Amherst since 1978.

Agnes Cox Campbell went into the motel business three times before 1961. After selling the first motel, she owned a poultry farm and yarn shop to support herself and two children. At the age of 70 she set up a third motel at Mariposa. She was a pupil at the Berkeley School for three years after she enrolled an oral school. *"To be a success one must be willing to work hard!"* she quoted.

Agencies

Marcella M. Meyer, Executive Director of the Greater Los Angeles Council on Deafness (GLAD), is one of the few deaf women in the United States to hold such a position.

Marcella Meyer

In spite of the pressures of her position, she is still a family person and delights in her three daughters and five grandchildren.

Marcella, who would like to see other deaf women take the reins *in all types of organizations, says, "Being a woman and an executive is no longer the impossible dream."* She is also President of the California Assn. of the Deaf, and was appointed a delegate to the California State Democratic Convention in 1987.

Mary Max Brown is on the managerial staff of the California Relay Service that began services on January 1, 1987.

A former Miss CAD Queen, she won the crown at the 1962 California Association of the Deaf Convention, held in San Diego.

Katherine Jankowski is another example of a successful administrator. She was employed as the program coordinator of DeafPride, Inc.

She left the agency in 1987 to pursue her studies for a doctorate in Communication Arts within Women's Studies. She commented that her work with Deaf Women United had convinced her that a strong self-help, self-empowering

Katherine "Kathy" Jankowski. Courtesy of Deaf Women United.

network is needed, especially since there is a general under-employment of deaf women.

Kathy, one of the recipients of the 1987 Outstanding Young Women of America award, is the coordinator of the Elderhostel program at Gallaudet University.

Marla Hatrak, from Indiana, was the first person to be the Manager of Special Services at the U.S. Capitol. Her responsibilities were to help deaf people get sign/oral interpreters, blind people get brailled information, people in wheelchairs find ramps, and even give "lost" visitors directions.

Marla moved to Los Angeles in 1987 to become Assistant Deputy Director at GLAD.

"Most people know nothing about deafness and deaf people," writes Marla. *"What surprised me the most was how people reacted to me as a deaf person. They were surprised that I was so—normal!"*

Cosmetology

With training at the Ohio School and meeting the State Board of Cosmetology requirements, **Reba Ward Booher,** was licensed and took over her mother's beauty shop in Springfield, Ohio. She operated it for 37 years before selling out and retiring to St. Augustine, Florida in the early '80s.

Only a few deaf women have become owners and/or operators of beauty parlors. In 1961, **Gladys O. Farrell Pauley** ran her own shop in White Sulphur Springs, West Virginia, and also **Fannie Bove** in Trenton, New Jersey.

Shelby Christian Kubis of Mary-

land, was the first deaf student from the Virginia School in Staunton, to be licensed in Cosmetology in 1957. At 16, Shelby worked at the school beauty shop on Saturdays and evenings styling hair for teachers and staff members. She is currently an instructor at KDES.

Robin Ching, an Art major at Cal-State, Northridge, is now a professional high-style beautician in the DC area.

Shortly after World War I, **Irene Castle,** half of the Vernon and Irene Castle dance team, started a new hair style. The women rushed to have their hair cut "bob style." Deaf women were late in following the style because, at first, their parents and/or husbands would not let them.

Federal

Edna Paananen Adler, a consultant for the deaf and the hard-of-hearing, has worked for the United States Government for more than 20 years. She was graduated from the Michigan School and from Gallaudet and is an advocate for deaf women in America to work together and become leaders. Her favorite saying is *"There is room in the world for deaf female leaders and for deaf heroines aspiring to the heights."*

Edna is the recipient of an honorary Doctor of Laws degree from Gallaudet College in 1980. Honors from a number of other organizations include: the National Association of the Deaf Distinguished Service Award, World Federation of the Deaf Decoration of Merit, Deaf Woman of the Year from Quota International, and the American Deafness

Edna P. Adler. Gallaudet Photo Lab.

and Rehabilitation Association Award for her dedication and support.

It gives her honor as the first woman to have a top job in the United States Government on Capital Hill. She went to public school until sixth grade. Her deafness from spinal meningitis was discovered at the age of ten.

Petra Fandrem Howard, of Minnesota, was a pioneer in Labor and Vocational Rehabilitiation departments beginning in the '40s. Gallaudet honored her with an honorary doctorate in 1960.

Pat Johanson, from Oregon, earned both a B.S. in Psychology and a Master's in Public Administration from Brigham Young University in Utah. She did her six-month internship in Washington, D.C., learning all about legislation relating to the handi-

capped. She is working on a Ph.D in Public Administration at George Washington University and was the Staff Director of the Commission on Education of the Deaf.

Pat was interviewed by the editor of *World Around You*, a nationally published newsletter for elementary school children. Commented Pat, *"Like many deaf people who learn signs as an adult, it was a shock to me. I was surprised at how much I had missed all my life."*

She is presently serving as coordinator of the Professional and Community Training Program in the College for Continuing Education National Academy.

Cheryl Kent, during the early 1980s, was a civil rights specialist with the U.S. Dept. of Housing and Urban Development (HUD), Office of Fair Housing and Equal Opportunity. She was an advocate for the handicapped.

"I had always thought that I was a loner by choice, but at Gal-

Petra F. Howard

laudet,"* said Cheryl, *"I realized that I was outgoing."*

In the 1980s, **Brenda Smith Keller**, of Maryland, became the Postal Supervisor at Gallaudet. She manages the staff of three full-time people and several temporary student helpers.

In the historic Georgetown area of Washington, D.C., stands out the Old Stone House built in 1765. It is a National Park, and a deaf Park Ranger, **Cathy Lennon Ingrams**, of Pennsylvania, gives tours in sign language for deaf visitors to observe the women baking goods over an open hearth, exhibit the basketweaving, rughooking, quilting just like the colonists did.

Robin Greene is a tour guide at the Federal Bureau of Investigation building in Washington, D.C. She lectures in sign language with a voice interpreter.

Industry

Thanks to World Wars I and II, the capabilities of deaf women have been recognized and the deafness is forgotten.

During World War I, deaf women in Akron, Ohio, built giant-sized gas balloons for England's defense against German planes. Again, during World War II, deaf women built more balloons to be moored along the Pacific Coast in preparation for the Japanese invasion which never occurred.

During World War II, deaf women were hired by defense plants to build airplanes, tanks, ships, and other war material. They were required to wear pants and headscarves (snoods) for safety purposes.

Sarah Wallace Fouts was the first deaf person to be hired at the Naval Avionic Center in Indianapolis, thus paving the way for more than 25 deaf workers during World War II.

Mercedes "Dee" Mayberry (Blankenship), a product of the Montana School, was the first deaf female member of the International Typographical Union (ITU). Dee started her printing career in the 1940s by traveling from town to town (often without pay for room-and-board, working for the experience).

According to the Gallaudet Encyclopedia, before the 1950s, the largest source of employment opportunities for deaf women was in the garment industry. Since then, deaf women have been moving out of blue collar work and into white collar jobs, including professional jobs (primarily teaching) and clerical work.

Legal

There have been, in past centuries, unjust and cruel laws dealing with deaf people. In the Western world, most of these repressive laws have been expunged, but a few still remain on the books.

The most prevalent and severely limiting laws were those forbidding the deaf:

• to marry among themselves;
• to obtain any jobs or positions in the government;
• to drive automobiles;
• to use sign language;
• to teach deaf children.

Sheila Conlon-Mentkowski, from Massachusetts, earned her M.A. from Gallaudet in 1974. She applied to at least 13 law schools

Top: Sheila Conlon-Mentkowski. Gallaudet Photo Lab.

Bottom: Dinah Moss Estes, first deaf juror in Alabama—1988.

around the country, was accepted by several and finally chose Georgetown. At present she is a lawyer with NORCAL, an agency for the deaf in Sacramento, California, after working eight years with the National Center for Law and the Deaf in Washington, D.C.

"Seeing other kids together made me feel marooned in deafness," avers Sheila. *"I missed out on the games, the gossip, all the girlish escapades."*

Training to be a lawyer was a challenging process for her.

"All Deaf-Mutes are Imbeciles"

In 1927, an investigation by the Dept. of the Interior, Bureau of Indian Affairs, found that Margaret Good, former student at Oklahoma School for the Deaf and a full-blooded Osage of Tulsa, Oklahoma, was being defrauded of her inheritance by her guardian, a lawyer.

Mr. Lafe Hubler, her guardian, was sworn as a witness and made a statement that she was insane and an imbecile because she was a deaf mute, and was not different from any other deaf mute, and in his opinion all deaf mutes were insane, mentally unbalanced and imbeciles.

The court found her mentally balanced and ordered that she be placed in some institution and under competent physicians familiar with the treatments of deafness, where her condition might be improved. A new guardian was appointed for her and her estate.

Carroll Robin Massey has been an advocate for the rights of deaf Native Americans. She is part Cherokee, and feels a special affinity with native Americans. She spent the summer of 1987 in Arizona to learn of their special needs.

Huberta Schroedel, the winner of the 1986 Durfee Foundation Award, is the founder and Executive Director of the New York Center for Law and the Deaf (1981). She was also the first deaf teacher to obtain a teaching license to work within the New York City school system. She received her early education at St. Mary's School for the Deaf in Buffalo, N.Y.

Joan K. Berke, of Flushing, N.Y., has been active in fighting for the rights of the disabled. She is a member of the New York Center for Law and the Deaf and New York Law School's Disability Rights Committee. She chairs the Consumer Education Committee in New York City. Her daughter, **Lisa Berke,** conducts the self-defense classes to deaf women in the Los Angeles area and workshop participants at the state and national levels sponsored by Los Angeles Commission on Assaults Against Women.

Amy Rowley, of New York, was a deaf elementary school student when her case for the right to a sign language interpreter in a public school was taken to the U.S. Supreme Court where it was defeated. Her parents, Nancy and Clifford, are deaf. Her mother, Nancy M. Rowley, won three medals (gold, silver and bronze) in swimming events at the Olympics in Helsinki, Finland.

Ruth Ann Lally Schornstein, of New Jersey, brought suit before the U.S. District Court in New Jersey during the '70s. She claimed discrimination because the college she was attending refused to pro-

vide paid interpreter services. The court decision upheld her. Many similar cases were later brought up and won in other states.

Susan Grappe is a police officer in New Orleans. She has Carbon, a trained Signal Dog, that responds to noises to help her. She decided to be a cop herself because of a bad prior experience with the police.

Mary Jean Sevoolish Moore, general attorney at the Office of Review and Appeals of the Equal Employment Opportunity Commission in Washington, D.C. was one of the ten outstanding handicapped federal employees honored in 1987 and she is one of 15 deaf attorneys in the United States.

Bonnie Tucker, an oralist lawyer, is with a Phoenix Law Firm. In 1985 she was elected chairwoman of the 12-member Arizona Council for the Deaf.

Jan Lou Jones of Spartanburg, South Carolina, graduated from the South Carolina School of Law in 1987, was the first deaf person to pass the South Carolina Bar examination.

Celia Burg Warshawsky, a native of New Jersey, was the first hearing-impaired person to interpret at a criminal trial in Illinois. She was named the International Deaf-Woman-of-the-Year at the convention in Atlanta, Georgia, in 1983.

State

Judith Viera Tingley of Oakland, California had the highest state level administrative position in California. She was the Program Manager, Deaf Services, California Department of Rehabilitation with

an office in Sacramento. In 1987 she started with a business firm after a one-year fellowship in Business Administration at Gallaudet. Judy was the first Social and Cultural Development Specialist at NTID and was also program director of the Hearing-Impaired Center at American River College (Sacramento, CA.), before she went to the Department of Rehabilitation.

Barbara Jean Wood was appointed in April, 1986, by Governor Michael Dukakis as the Commissioner of the Massachusetts Commission for the Deaf and Hard of Hearing. One of her duties is managing a million-dollar-plus budget for a 30-plus staff. She was the keynote speaker at the second DWU Conference in 1987.

She was listed one of the city's 100 interesting women in the *Boston Woman* magazine (March, 1988) in their annual "Salute to Boston's dynamic achievers." She hailed from Scotch Plains, New Jersey.

Barbara Jean Wood

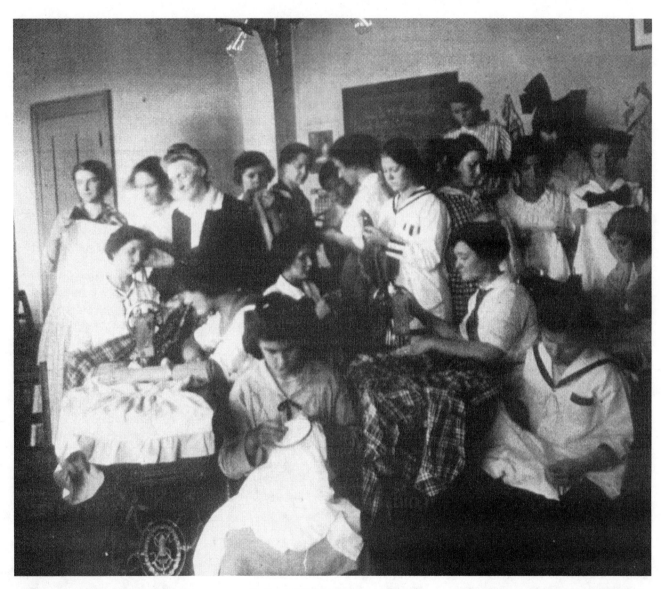

Barbara Babbini Brasel has been the Director of the Connecticut Commission of the Deaf and Hard-of-Hearing for several years. She formerly was a community leader in California, taught at Cal-State University, Northridge, and was invited to many federally supported workshops and conferences during President Lyndon B. Johnson's years.

Catherine Nash, a graduate of Syracuse University (B.A. in English and Library Science) and University of Hartford (M.Ed.) is the 1980s Educational Projects Co-ordinator, Connecticut Commission on the Deaf and Hearing-Impaired.

Above: At Kentucky Asylum for the Tuition of the Deaf and Dumb—1916. It became the first state-supported school west of the Allegheny Mountains in Danville. A bill was introduced by a state senator who had a deaf daughter, Lucy Barbee. Courtesy of Gallaudet Archives.

Opposite: At New Jersey School for the Deaf (now Marie H. Katzenbach School), ca 1949. Courtesy of Gallaudet Archives.

Communication

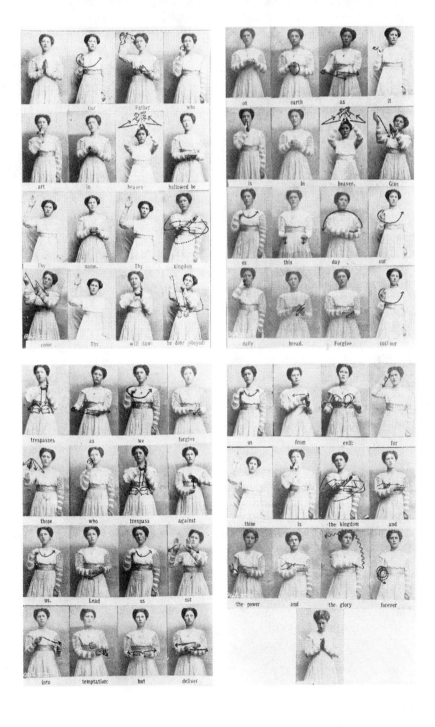

The Lord's Prayer

COMMUNICATION

estural communication has a long history in human behavior. It was probably used before spoken language developed. As early as 386 B.C., Socrates commented on how the deaf use gestures to communicate.

Manuscripts from the 10th Century show manual systems which were used to represent numbers and as memory aids. An old Italian manuscript illustrates numbers from one to one million.

Gestures were important to Renaissance speakers. Renaissance paintings show the use of gestures in debate.

Symbolic gestures of Japanese Buddhists express religious and philosophic ideas.

Folklorists made studies of gestures used in Italy, India, Shanghai and other places in the world.

Early manual alphabets are well recorded but illustrations of early gestural signs are lacking.

In the Middle Ages monks made vows of a life of silence, communicating only through fingerspelling.

It is presumed that in the early years deaf people in America developed their own signs.

American Indians have their own "independent or original" method of communication.

Thomas H. Gallaudet brought Laurent Clerc, a young Frenchman who was deaf and an instructor of the deaf. Through Clerc, French Sign Language was introduced to America in 1816.

Like all living languages, the vocabulary of American Sign Language (ASL) has increased in volume through the decades.

Previous page. The Lord's Prayer as photographed and illustrated by Ella F. Blank. Gallaudet Photo Lab.

Carol Padden. Gallaudet Photo Lab.

On Martha's Vineyard everyone used sign language as far back as 1715, according to an October, 1980, article in *The Deaf American* by anthropologist Nora Grace.

"The popular belief that speech and lip-reading is the salvation of all the deaf is to be regretted," said Alice Taylor Terry, a California feminist of the 1920s. *"By means of sign language we, the deaf, have platform speaking, lectures, sermons, and plays, which lip-reading cannot give us."* She is further quoted in a 1925 issue of *The Silent Worker, "Besides, it is the manual method of communication which removed completely all sense of isolation from the deaf."*

One of the earliest sign language books published in America was photographed and illustrated by Ella F. Black (d. 1954) in 1918. While teaching at Iowa School for the Deaf, she photographed and illustrated vocabulary of signs used in her husband, John Schuyler

Long's book, *The Sign Language: A Manual of Signs Illustrated.* The book was reprinted in 1944, 1949 and again in 1952.

Dr. Carol Padden is a well-known lecturer who presents workshops and seminars on sign language and linguistics all across the country. She is an associate professor in the Department of Communication at the University of California, San Diego. Carol is the co-author of several books, including *A Basic Course in American Sign Language, ASL: A Look at Its History, Structure & Community,* and *Deaf in America: Voices from a Culture.*

"Deaf People feel a strong identification with ASL since it is a part of their cultural background," stated Carol, *"but when they are involved in community activities, the use of another language allows them to interact with others who are not deaf."*

Ella Mae Lentz is a pioneer in ASL instruction. She has taught ASL, structure of ASL, and creative uses of ASL at several colleges. She is noted for presentations of her original poetic and dramatic works in ASL. She credits her interest in story-telling to her deaf mother, Mary Ellen, who stimulated her during her childhood.

Ella currently teaches ASL at Ohlone Community College in Fremont, California. She is the co-author of a newly published sign language curriculum, *Signing Naturally: The Vista American Sign Language Series.*

Elaine Linder Shaffer was the first to teach sign language classes

Ella Mae Lentz at Spectrum in Austin, Texas—1976.

in San Jose, Calif., beginning on January 6, 1964.

Betty-Jo Raines Lependorf, of California, was the first deaf person to be certified by the State Board of Education. She received a "Standard Designated Subjects Teaching Credential" for Finger-spelling and Sign Language in the early 1960s.

Betty-Jo was instrumental in starting sign language classes in adult schools in Albany, Berkeley, Oakland, San Leandro, San Lorenzo, Hayward, and Livermore. She was also a special consultant to the California School for the Deaf in Berkeley to train hearing members of the staff and faculty in the language of signs.

Martina Jo "MJ" Bienvenu, born to deaf parents in Baton Rouge, Louisiana, was the first recipient of the Stokoe Scholarship. Since 1978, she conducted numerous workshops on ASL, ASL training, nonverbal communication, attitudes in the deaf community, deaf culture and the semantics of

ASL to parents, professionals of the deaf, deaf people and interpreters. After working in the book department at NAD and at Gallaudet Bookstore for a number of years, she transferred to Kendall School where she was a Communication Specialist in Sign Language. She worked part-time for the National Interpreting Training Consortium for one semester and at the Linguistic Research Laboratory in 1980 as a research assistant while majoring in linguistics in graduate school. She is currently at the Bicultural Center with Betty Colomonos.

Barbara Marie Kannapell of Kentucky and Indiana, born into a deaf family — her parents, uncle and two aunts — worked seventeen years as research assistant following her graduation from Gallaudet in Gallaudet College's Office of

Institutional Research. Then she, a linguistic specialist, transferred to the Instructional Development and Evaluation Center. She was the first person to earn a PhD in Sociolinguistics at Georgetown University.

She travels widely as a lecturer on various topics ranging from advocacy to bilingual education for deaf children. *"I notice many schools like the idea of using the term total communication. I notice many teachers speaking and signing at the same time, but that is all. I think total communication means using other methods, including ASL. ASL is used by deaf people throughout the U.S. If you include ASL, then I think that is the true meaning of total communication."* Quotes are excerpted from Chapter 5 from *"A Handful of Stories,"* by Roslyn Rosen, project coordinator.

Elaine Lynn Jacobowitz, a graduate of Lexington School, New York City, wrote and directed a full-length play, *Oh Stop . . . Oh Stop* based on deaf experiences living in a dormitory. It was well received by Gallaudet Alumni during the June, 1982, reunion.

A doctoral candidate at the Virginia Polytechnic Institute and State University School of Instructional Technology, Lynn has been traveling extensively. Her lectures and workshops focus on the latest technology and materials to be used in teaching ASL and deaf culture.

Her new book on cartoons reflects deaf people's lives from 1880 to the present. Hearing people with little or no knowledge of sign language may not be able to appreciate fully these jokes

E. Lynn Jacobowitz. Gallaudet Photo Lab.

about deaf people's experiences, handshapes stories, cultural information and sign puns that can often lose their essence in voice translation.

She supervises the Sign Language Instruction for Gallaudet employees program. *"Unless children are provided with all possible opportunities to communicate effectively in school environments,"* she writes, *"they will forever be second-class citizens."*

Barbara Sanderson Babbini Brasel was the first sign language teacher to develop a professional and marketable student textbook with a teacher's manual. She

Barbara Kannapell. Gallaudet Photo Lab.

is now Executive Director of the Connecticut Commission for the Deaf and Hearing Impaired. She also made a series of 8mm loop movies in the late '60s that were distributed to sign language teachers around the nation by the NAD.

Jane Kelleher, a former Miss Deaf Iowa, gave lectures on *Recent Developments in ASL Literature*. She was visiting Assistant Professor and Acting Director of Sign Language Programs at the Northeastern University in Boston. She was the chairwoman of the Sign Communication Department at Gallaudet University before moving to Hawaii in 1987.

The Salk Institute in La Jolla, California, employed **Bonnie Gough** to help with American Sign Language (ASL) Research studies at the beginning. There have since been about 20 deaf women assisting with the program through the years. To name a few: **Carlene Canady Pedersen, Ella Mae Lentz, Carol Padden, Jane Norman, Cinnie Kuntze, Monica Schuester, Maureen O'Grady, Freda Norman,** and **Cindy O'Grady.** They are all from deaf families. **Dorothy Squire Miles,** of the British Isles, was one of the earlier research assistants.

Debbie Rennie (Clown Zabami) is known in the Rochester, New York area for her ASL story-telling skill — children's stories from fairy tales to ghosts and horrors.

Mrs. "Teethman"

In Philadelphia, the principal stopped by **Shirley Holtzman Glassman's** evening sign language class to check on attendance and mentioned an article in a magazine about Koko, the gorilla who knows 375 signs. Shirley couldn't resist the temptation: *"See, now the gorilla knows more signs than you do!"*

Shirley Glassman, a teacher's aide at New Jersey's Marie Katzenbach School for the Deaf, was asked to take a freshman high school class to the library. The teacher introduced her to the students by using the signs for "glass" (touching the teeth) and "man" for her name.

She is now known to one and all as "Mrs. Teethman."

Shirley was an assistant director of the *Radio TTY* Program at the Pennsylvania School during the early 1970s. Each day a local team took United Press news of the world and the nation, edited it, added news about the deaf community and put it on a TTY tape. Using a TTY tape reader, the signals were phoned to an FM transmitter located at Temple University radio station. Deaf people in the area with special FM radios could receive the broadcast TTY signals and obtain print-out of the news on their TTY machines. Ham radio operators used radio TTY for many years.

"Do Not Touch"

Stopping by to visit the Carlsbad Caverns in New Mexico, Ray and Carola **Rasmus,** of Fremont, California, noticed the large signs reminding the tourists not to touch the beautiful forms of stalactites and stalagmites.

With awe, the family talked the way deaf people usually do, with big signs and much pointing.

Two park rangers approached and threatened to throw them out if they did not stop touching nature's beauty in the cavern. Carola was embarrassed but decided to confront the rangers, saying, *"we were simply talking, not touching anything."* The rangers apologized and let them enjoy the rest of the tour.

Community Services

Margaret E. Jackson of New York City was the chairwoman of the event in the U.S. and Canada that resulted in an avalanche of boxes of clothing and food that overwhelmed Marguerite Colas. Funds from the sale of stamps ensured the continuation of the work at the Centre. In 1949 she received a citation. This honor was in recognition of her work for the relief of deaf French children.

Marguerite Colas, founded and was director of the Centre Societe du Sourds-Muets in Paris, France. She and American deaf artist Kelly Stevens arranged for the sale of De l'Epee commemorative stamps prior to World War II to raise funds for the Centre.

The Sunshine Circle, a non-sectarian organization of deaf ladies of Los Angeles, organized in 1913, is still in existence. The members of The Sunshine Circle put in much time cheering the sick and providing financial aid for worthy causes.

The Fairy Godmothers Club in Philadelphia was active during World War I. It was an offshoot of the American Red Cross. The club raised funds to aid deaf refugees of the war zone in Europe.

Elizabeth "Betty" Broecker was known as the champion of the deaf in Philadelphia in the 1970s. She was the program coordinator of Community Services for the Deaf which was founded by Gallaudet College.

The program was a 15-month pilot project designed to *"bring the deaf community into a more*

Previous page. Unit of production workers of the Red Cross at Lexington School—1942. Courtesy of Gallaudet Archives.

Margaret E. Jackson

compatible atmosphere with the rest of society."

While serving as Assistant Director of Public Relations at Gallaudet, she tried to "educate" the public about deafness.

Betty emphasized in newspaper articles that *"One learns to talk by imitating. Since the deaf person, in many cases, has never heard words, he doesn't know how to use his instrument of speech."*

She hoped that the term "deaf-mute" and its counterpart, "deaf-and-dumb" would be discarded by the press since both expressions convey a misconception of what deaf people are really like.

The Omega Chapter of Phi Kappa Zeta (PKZ) in the San Francisco Bay Area held a fund-raising event, *Casino/Roaring '20s* in 1986. The profit was over $4,000 and half of it went to the National Captioning Institute. The balance was divided among deaf senior citizen groups, the deaf-blind organization and the CSD *Close-Up* program.

Nancy V. Becker was stricken with multiple sclerosis. Her family and friends give her full support and she can continue with her activities in and for the community. She is always willing to share her experiences about MS and deafness and how to live with them.

"I just don't know everything about multiple sclerosis (MS), but I understand it a lot better," says Nancy. *"Being deaf doesn't bother me in the least, but having MS is something new for me to learn to cope with and accept." "I just need a little extra time to spend learning about my 'new legs',"* meanwhile keeping her life going just as it always has," she continued.

"I can't afford to waste time. There is so much yet to experience—so many new challenges to take on—so why waste time with self-pity?" And with a determined look, she said *"As my deafness isn't an obstacle in my path, neither will MS be an obstacle."*

Nancy V. Becker

Gina Oliva and Sue Gill-Gould at Dance for Heart benefit. Gallaudet Photo Lab.

E. Hortense "Horty" Henson Auerbach of Maryland, was elected President of the Senior Citizens Section of the NAD in 1982. Charlotte Collums, of Arkansas, was chosen as her assistant.

Hortense initiated the Tutorial Center at Gallaudet University. Since her retirement in the 1980s, she has given many, many hours of volunteer work at NAD Headquarters. At the 1986 NAD Convention in Salt Lake City, she was honored with both the Golden Rose Award and the Flying Fingers Award.

Mary Frances "Muffy" Miller Brightwell, daughter of a state senator of Missouri, said, *"The deaf will find painting a wonderful hobby if they have the inner ability and work to develop it. Everybody will work hard to increase awareness about deaf culture and the need to preserve it."* Reprinted from *"On the Green,"* Vol. 18.

Townspeople in Pasadena, California, learned about deafness from working with her in many civic activities. She is an amateur artist and she has often donated her prize-winning art pieces to charity benefits. They opened up their home for weekly swim parties where hearing parents and sign language class students could practice signs with the deaf community.

Sisters Ruth David Phillips and Grace Davis Mudgett are known as popular "gals" at various conventions of the deaf. Ruth in Laurel, Maryland and Grace in Jacksonville, Illinois, both retirees, are doing volunteer charitable work for the deaf communities. Their cousin, Hazel Davis, does similiar work in the San Francisco Bay Area. Their fathers were teachers at the Texas School for the Deaf in Austin.

The Christine MacIntyre Memorial Scholarship by the International Dance-Exercise Association awarded Gina Oliva, who worked at the Gallaudet as workout instructor. She specializes in aerobics. Ellie Korres joined the staff, teaching body conditioning classes in both sign language and voice with music.

Pauline Nathanson Peikoff was the driving force behind the Centennial Fund for Gallaudet College that her husband David conducted. She was honored with a *Service to Others Award* during the festivities of Gallaudet University Week in 1986. They both were educated in Canada.

Pauline "Polly" Peikoff. Gallaudet Photo Lab.

Sarah W. Fouts lived near the *Indy-500* speedway in Indianapolis. She and her busband often opened their house to race drivers and their wives, providing them with a "home away from home." This was before suitable accommodations were built in that area. There were barracks for the male drivers but no suitable lodgings for their wives.

Beatrice Davis of Chicago is known as the raffle-selling champion, having collected over $24,000 for the NAD during the summer of 1986. She also received the *Golden Rose Award* at the 1986 Salt Lake City NAD Convention. Beatrice once remarked: *"A book about deaf women is long overdue and when one is out, it should be on the 'must read' list for all deaf women — and for men as well."*

Pat Wilson Zinkovich, of California, was a mail carrier delivering mail door-to-door in her mukluks during her residency in Fairbanks, Alaska, in the 1960s. She was honored with a 1986 *Woman Helping Women* award by the International Soroptimist Club in Oakland, California, in 1986.

Wendy Whitting Laird from New York City has been an instrumental supporter at the New England Home for the Deaf where her husband, Eddy, is the director. She also gave her time as the director of several Miss Deaf Massachusetts pageants. Her father was the Pastor of St. Anne's Church in New York City.

Louise Hume. Reprinted from **The Silent Worker.**

Louise Hume has contributed a large part of her retirement years to conducting educational programs for deaf patients in various Ohio State institutions. These programs are supported by the Mental Health Association.

The Silent Worker in 1949 lauded Louise of Akron, Ohio as a champion recruiter. She had persuaded 466 people to become members of the NAD; secured 118 renewals and 20 life members single-handedly.

A product of the Oregon School for the Deaf, **Georgia Ward Morikawa** is the Chairwoman of the Hawaii State Coordinating Council on Deafness [similiar to other states' Commissions on Deafness]. Georgia was the first woman selected as Hawaii's Outstanding Volunteer-of-the-Year in 1977 by the wife of Hawaii's governor. She has held various offices in many organizations in Hawaii and is a board member of several agencies serving the handicapped in the Island State.

Rachel Stone-Harris, from North Carolina, is the co-chairperson of the Deaf Way Program. This international festival and conference on the language, culture, and history of deaf people from all over the world is being held July 9-14, 1989, in Washington, D.C. It is sponsored by Gallaudet University with endorsements from the World Federation of the Deaf and the National Association of the Deaf. Rachel feels that the Deaf Way *"will prove to be contagious, and everybody will work hard to increase awareness about deaf culture and the need to preserve it."* Reprinted from *"On the Green,"* Vol. 18.

Alberta Delozier Smith, of Knoxville, Tennessee, where she began her teaching career in 1950, went to Australia for the International Quota Club Women-of-the-Year award. Her daughter was invited along to interpret for her. She retired in 1987. Communication with both deaf and hearing persons was her forte, as evidenced by her position as Chairperson of the Knoxville Area Communication Center Board of Directors where she focused on reduction of telephone rates for TDD long distance calls and her testimony before the Public Service Commission on this issue. Besides rearing four children as a single parent and her activities with state and national associations of the deaf, Alberta managed to find time to serve on various committees.

Deaf-Blind

DEAF-BLIND

During the early civilizations of the Greeks and Romans, the needs of the deaf-blind and other disabled groups were neglected. They were often treated with cruelty and were left on the streets to beg.

As the Christianity movement advanced, people's attitudes changed. At first the church took in disabled people and provided for their material needs. It is believed that William the Conqueror established shelters for them in atonement for his sins.

In 1250 an institution was established in Paris for blinded Crusaders. Interest in their education spread throughout Europe.

Samuel Gridley Howe (1801–1876), was the founder and director of the Perkins Institution for the Blind in Boston. He was a strong advocate of oralism when he made his first attempt to teach **Laura Dewey Bridgman** (1829–1889), a deaf-blind student. Eventually she learned to talk to people by tapping letters and/or finger-spelling in manual alphabet on their hands.

Laura D. Bridgman

Hellen Keller, talking to a group of World War II deafened soldiers at Borden General Hospital in Oklahoma, ca 1946. Courtesy of Gallaudet Archives.

Anne Sullivan (1866–1936) was a partially blind student who learned how to read braille from Laura. Some years later, she took a train with Laura's gift (doll) to visit six-year-old Helen Keller in Alabama.

Before Helen Keller was two years old, brian fever took away her sight, hearing and speech. Anne Sullivan became Helen's tutor and companion for more than fifty years. Anne and her former husband, John Macy, the writer, helped Helen finish her first book, *"The Story of My Life,"* in 1903. It was translated in more than fifty languages. Helen went to Radcliffe, from which she graduated with honors in 1904. Anne stayed with her through these years interpreting lectures and class discussions.

Previous page. Alexander Graham Bell interpreting for Helen Keller at the 4th American Association for the Promotion of Teaching Speech to the Deaf–1894. Courtesy of Gallaudet Archives.

After college, Helen became active at American Foundation for the Blind. She donated monies from the book to help soldiers who were blinded in World War I. After the war ended, Helen and Anne made a movie of Helen's life, *"Helen Keller in Her Story,"* in Hollywood. To make a living, they did many stage shows in many cities.

"The problems of deafness," stated Miss Keller, *"are more complex, if not more important than those of blindness. After a lifetime in silence and darkness, I find that to be deaf is a greater affliction than to be blind."*

The oral advocates continued to claim Helen's accomplishments were due largely to speech and lipreading. Her lifelong companion, Anne Sullivan, gave the credit to the effective use of the manual alphabet.

On Helen's 65th birthday, a special department—services for the deaf-blind—was formed at the Industrial Home for the Blind (IHB). Sixteen years later a new center—The Helen Keller National Center for Deaf-Blind Youths and Adults—was built on federal government-donated property at Sands Point, Long Island, New York in 1971.

Helen did not live to see it but her dream for a national program for the deaf-blind was fulfilled. It was realized during the term of Mary Switzer, the Secretary of Health, Education and Welfare.

A "Declaration of Rights of Deaf-Blind People" was adopted September, in New York City at the historic first Helen Keller World Conference on Services to Deaf-Blind Youths and Adults.

Helen May Martin (1893–1947) was a deaf-blind graduate of the Kansas School for the Deaf. She became deaf at the age of eight and blind at 17. Her mother taught her how to feel vibration through her feet. Helen learned to play piano and performed music in sign language in churches. She earned her living from the making of hair swatches.

Lottie Sullivan, one of the deaf-blind students at the Colorado School School for the Deaf, won gold medals for her demonstration of school work at the 1904 St. Louis World's Fair. One of Lottie's teachers, Bessie Veditz, was the wife of George W. Veditz, the seventh president of the NAD.

Charlotte "Char" Whitacre, legally deaf-blind, is the 1980's advocate for her peers. She has conducted braille classes for victims of Usher's Syndrome and sign language classes for volunteers. She has served on the board of the

Charlotte Whitacre

American Association of the Deaf-Blind for several terms.

Char received the (1984) Dorothy Morrison Jacobs Memorial Community Award for her services to the community. She works part-time at DCARA as the referral agent for the deaf-blind in the Bay Area. In addition Char teaches classes at Ohlone College, Fremont CA. She shares her deaf-blind experiences with budding interpreters in the Ohlone program.

There is an apartment-motel complex in Los Angeles leased for deaf-blind adults. Muriel Hersom was the founder in the late 1960's and is still the proprietress.

Michelle Craig married Robert J. Smithdas, author of *Life at My Fingertips*. They are now with the Helen Keller National Center for Deaf-Blind Youths and Adults in Sand Point, New York. They are both deaf-blind and Michelle says they *"fell in love at first touch."*

"I wish I could tell families of deaf-blind people," said Michelle, *"that the most important thing*

they can do is to show love and acceptance."

Margaret Prescott Montaque published *Closed Doors: Studies of Deaf and Blind Children* in 1915. It was adapted by Walt Disney Studios in 1981 and a movie was made.

Kathleen Speer, in the early 1980's, was the first deaf-blind person to be successfully trained to use a guide dog.

Dee Follette of Sacramento, California, is another popular deaf-blind advocate. She speaks to school children and community groups in her area. Her talks take away pity and sadness replacing them with understanding and compassion.

One school boy wrote a thank you note adding, *"I am glad you came because now I understand better what a blind and/or deaf person feels but I will never completely understand."*

Another child wrote, *"One of the many things I learned was that you don't have to see and hear to make your way in this world."*

Jackie Coker, a deaf-blind counselor for the California State Department of Rehabilitation during the 1970's and 1980's, is known for her enthusiasm and hard work helping other deaf-blind people integrate into the mainstream society. She has been honored for her expertise by many service clubs and agencies in California.

Kathleen Potter , Founder and President of the Southern California Association of the Deaf-Blind, is very much involved in the Deaf-Blind World Recreation Association of the Deaf in the United States. She teaches sign language to blind people at the Braille Institute in Los Angeles.

Education

EDUCATION

"To instruct the deaf
No art could reach,
No care improve them
And no wisdom teach."
Written in 1 B.C.

In 355 B.C., Aristotle wrote: *"Men that are deaf are in all cases dumb."*

Note: Long ago the word "dumb" indicated loss of power to speak, or unable to speak. Over the years dumb has come to mean lack of intelligence. The hearing public refers more to the second definition: lack of intelligence when confronted by the phrase "deaf-and-dumb." The inability-to-speak concept has been lost over the years, leading to misconceptions within the hearing society. The deaf community seeks to remedy this misunderstanding.

One of the earliest recorded efforts in America to teach a deaf child was in Rowley, Massachusetts colony, in 1679. The neighbors thought that witches were involved and so officials ordered an investigation.

It was not until 1889 that the National Deaf-Mute College officially accepted women students. In 1886, arrangements were made to accommodate women students and the 1887–1889 academic years were declared an experimental period for them. While in those days women were supposed to be housewives or teachers, some did manage to study beyond the bachelor's degree. Nevertheless, it was not until 1970 that the first deaf woman is known to have earned a doctorate.

Ann Szymaposkie, one of the first women to enroll in the National Deaf-Mute College, ca 1864. Courtesy of the Szymaposkie family.

Previous page. Astrid A. Goodstein teaching class. Gallaudet Photo Lab.

Emily Lewis, the first female pupil at the Texas School for the Deaf, in the late 1860s, was later a teacher and principal of this school. She was the first deaf woman principal in America.

The Emily Lewis Dormitory at the Austin school is named in her honor.

The Kentucky School, in Danville, founded in 1823, was the first state-supported school. **Barbee Hall** is named for **Lucy Barbee**, the first student to be enrolled.

The **Mildred Middleton** Dormitory for older students, is named for a former housemother. Mildred and her husband had a total of 85 years on the campus.

Three buildings at the Indiana School for the Deaf were recently named in honor of four dedicated deaf women for their faithful years of service: **Ethel Koob** Dormitory; **Amy Fowler** and **Elizabeth Green** Health Center, and **Ola B. Brown** Cafeteria.

In 1890, Anson and Julie Halvorson Spears, graduates of the Minnesota School for the Deaf, were appointed superintendent and matron of the North Dakota School for the Deaf in Devil's Lake. The school opened with only one student, a girl. At the end of the first school year the enrollment had increased to a total of 23 students.

As of Fall 1988, there is still no deaf woman superintendent of a school for the deaf. However, many wives are giving male administrators their full support. They include: **Donna Englestrom Davila** at Gallaudet University, **MaryAnn DiCola Corson** at the Louisiana School for the Deaf, **Judie Stein Cronlund** at the New York State School for The Deaf, and **Frances May White** at the Oklahoma School for the Deaf.

The Depression Years
— Ruth Fish Clarke

During my senior year at Gallaudet (1931), I had an interview with the principal of the American School for the Deaf and applied for a teaching position to begin the following fall. There was no opening.

Since the American School had no courses in typing and business practice, I suggested that such courses be established. Hartford was the insurance capital of the world and there would be a need for trained typists and bookkeepers.

The principal stressed the fact that the country was in the midst of a depression and that ASD had no funds to purchase typewriters. I mentioned the fact that two members of the ASD Board of Directors were officials of the Royal typewriter and Underwood typewriter companies, then located in Hartford. I suggested that donations of used typewriters from either one or both companies could be made to ASD.

The principal thought my suggestion made sense and agreed to broach the subject to the officials of the two companies. Further, he would make recommendations for the board to establish the teaching of business practice to begin in the Fall of 1932.

It became a reality when I began my teaching career in business practice after taking post-graduate courses in business.

Ten years later, after having a son, I returned as an instructor in sewing, the position I held until I retired in 1972.

Ruth Fish Clarke

One day, out of the clear blue sky, the vocational supervisor informed me that I would teach sewing to a class of 12 boys. That caught me by surprise! This was something new. Boys! A challenge!

Imagine the awkward situation when the boys entered the classroom. Some were uneasy and asked if they were going to be making feminine things. They were assured that it would not be so.

Noticing one of the boys was missing a button on his shirt, I asked him to come forward and stand before the class. I pointed out the area of the missing button and then explained to the class that some day after they left school they might be living away from home. Then the training they received in the class in sewing and mending would be useful to them. There were amused smiles.

What to do the first week the

boys were in class? I taught them names of the parts of boys shirts, trousers, etc; taught them sewing of scraps of cloth as a prelude to mending torn clothing.

One day a youngster brought a pillow case full of clothing that needed sewing and mending. He stated that his mother wanted me (the teacher) to do the repairing. No way would I permit that! The poor fellow was kept busy for several weeks making his own repairs.

Ten years later the same fellow came to me at a social event and thanked me for the valuable training he obtained.

One day in the '30s, all the deaf teachers at the Indiana School for the Deaf were called to a meeting with the principal. Some parents complained of having deaf teachers teaching their children, a common complaint in those days. She, the Principal, mentioned her belief that hearing teachers were being paid more because they could teach better than deaf teachers.

That infuriated me. I felt like walking out but I could not afford to then. Some single deaf females said, *"Well, I'm thankful to have a job."*

—Mary Blackinton Ladner

In the 1930's, during the depression years, many schools for the deaf had problems with budget cuts from their states. One school wanted both husband and wife to teach but the budget allowed only the husband. Then the superintendent had a bright idea — he reduced the husband's salary to pay the wife's.

Augusta K. Barrett, a deaf teacher, tells of an incident at the teachers' convention at Morganton, N.C. in 1922.

Someone on the platform declared that all the deaf could learn to lip-read lectures and chapel addresses. The subject was then declared open for discussion.

About 60 deaf people, among them a number of expert lip-readers, were in the audience. Urged by friends to respond to the challenge, Augusta went to the platform. An expert lip-reader herself, she spoke orally, saying it was impossible for most deaf to lip-read lectures, and asked the convention if they could read her lips, speaking without voice.

Edith Mansford Fitzgerald

In her time, and for many years afterward, **Edith Mansford Fitzgerald** (1877–1940) was recognized as one of the leading educators of the deaf. She devised the Fitzgerald Key, a simplified method of teaching sentence structure to deaf children. It is still used in many schools for the deaf throughout the country. She was also the author of *Straight Language for the Deaf* in 1926.

She said, *"Peter, Peter, Pumpkin Eater, had a wife and couldn't keep her."* She then asked if anyone had read her lips. The hearing teachers as well as the expert lip-readers all had to admit their inability to read a single word.

Try this sentence yourself, looking in a mirror, and you will see how difficult it is to read, although it is a phrase almost everyone has known since childhood.

By this simple demonstration, the lady had stumped the August convention of teachers.

Donna Drake

Donna Drake, of a deaf family in Arkansas, has served the first deaf woman supervising teachers at the Florida School for the Deaf in St. Augustine. She has served on the Gallaudet University Alumni Association Board many terms during the 1970's and 1980's.

Judith Mezzanote Gilliam, a graduate of Hartford's American School for the Deaf, has been on the Talladega (Alabama) Committee for the International Year of the Disabled. She received an award from the Pilot Club International for the *Most Outstanding Handicapped Professional Woman of the Year in 1985.* In 1975, after teaching deaf-blind students for several years, Judith became the first deaf woman to be a high school supervisor at the Alabama School for the Deaf.

Illinois' June E. Newkirk taught at the Arizona School for the Deaf & Blind, the University of Arizona and California State University at Northridge for some 40 years. She is known for her warm hospitality to students and visitors from far and near, exchanging information about deaf culture and education.

Sarah Stifler Val

Sarah Stifler Val from the Western Pennsylvania School for the Deaf at Pittsburgh, was the first deaf person to be employed at MSSD in the fall of 1969. Upon retirement as English professor in 1987, she volunteers at Children's Hospital and NAD. She was invited to speak at the metropolitan Washington Area Public Libraries celebrating the 200th birthday of Thomas H. Gallaudet during Deaf Heritage Week, December 6-12, 1987.

Ruby Miller Samples of South Bend, Indiana, Gallaudet 1947, was the first female deaf teacher in a public school, teaching hearing children back in the early 1950's in Niles, Michigan.

Frances Lupo was the first full-time deaf classroom teacher-supervisor for elementary and junior high school grades 1–8, during the 1950's through 1970's, at the Lexington School for the Deaf in New York.

Lutie Acuff, deaf aunt of Virginia Chambers Lange until her retirement in 1960, taught for 50 years at her alma mater, the Tennessee School for the Deaf.

Katherine Greene Holcomb, from Georgia, was the first woman President of the NTID Student Congress (NSC), 1983-84. Barbara Schell Bass from Idaho was the first of a long line of female presidents of the Gallaudet College Student Body Government (SBG):

Barbara Schell (Idaho)	1959–60
Ausma Smits (Illinois)	1960–61
Donna Drake (Arkansas)	1968–69
June Rotherberg (New York)	1973–74
Patricia Shores (Canada)	1983–84
Doris Wilding (Idaho)	1985–86

Residential Life

Ann Garretson Benedict of Cincinnati, has rich memories of her childhood days, thanks to her parents.

Her father, a columnist of The *Cincinnati Enquirer,* traveled world-wide, taking his wife with him. They sent Ann "away" to the Central Institute for the Deaf in St. Louis. Her parents felt guilty about this so they tried to make it up by showering Ann with many entertaining surprises. On one particular occasion a small circus group came to C.I.D. to perform for Ann and her friends. Another time a small plane flew around C.I.D. pulling a banner reading, "Happy Birthday Dearest Ann."

Roslyn "Roz" Rosen. Courtesy of Gallaudet Archives.

PL 94-142

Roslyn "Roz" Goodstein Rosen was the first co-ordinator of Gallaudet's PL 94-142 Program which developed publications and provided nation-wide training (1977–78). She then became director of Gallaudet's Kellogg *Special Schools of the Future* Program. Today, she continues as Gallaudet's first female Dean and directs the College for Continuing Education.

Under her direction, the workshops touched on every aspect of deafness, education, rehabilitation, home life and society. She has been active at both state and national levels of the NAD and has served on the National Captioning Institute Advisory Board.

"*Before PL 94-142 was in effect in 1976,*" writes Carol Arlen Harter, of Pittsburgh, "*I did not realize how difficult mainstreaming was for me without interpreters.*

Life became easier when I first learned sign language and attended classes at Gallaudet College in 1963 where teachers used sign language."

Cinda Lautenschlegar was the first deaf woman graduate of the College of Engineering with a BS degree in Mechanical Engineering at RIT-NTID (1987).

Continuing Education

Marge Klugman of Los Angeles, is an advocate for Adult Education classes.

In 1987, she became the first woman president of Temple Beth Solomons of the Deaf and has arranged many popular monthly panels on timely issues at the temple in Arleta, California.

Arkansas' Betty Bounds-Wood, the only deaf director of five Gallaudet Regional Centers in the United States, came to Fremont, California in 1987 with rich experiences. Upon her graduation from Gallaudet, she taught at the Governor Baxter School for the Deaf in

Betty Bounds-Wood

Maine before transferring to Western Oregon State College. There she was the associate professor who coordinated the interpreter training program." *It is definitely OK to be DEAF, even more so to be a WOMAN!,*" enthused Betty, "*and in being both, what a way to go!*"

Pauline Erina Spanbauer from Illinois, born to deaf parents, was the first female Peace Corps volunteer in the Philippines in 1974. After two years of service, she enrolled at NTID. She was the first recipient of the Best Actress Award at NTID theatre. Currently, she is a Eurythmics instructor at Kendall School.

Gloria Martinez, a 1985 graduate of Gallaudet College, majored in Business Administration/Accounting. She works for a federal savings and loan bank in Virginia.

Said Gloria, "*The community college provided note-takers, but I hated that because I never knew if I was missing something. So I would tape the lectures, and every evening my father would write out, word for word, the lectures from the tape.*

"*I felt sorry for him. He showed a father's labor of love when he worked all day and then spent every evening doing that for me,*" she remembered. "*I tried another college and it was the same thing. Then I found out about VR and Gallaudet College.*"

Opposite: Pauline Spanbauer, Peace Corps Volunteer with the students at the Southeast Asian Institute for the Deaf in Quezon City, Philippines.

Deaf Women with Earned Doctorates

(courtesy of Jack Gannon of "Deaf Heritage")

1970 Nansie Sharpless, Ph.D.,
Wayne State U.
1970 Judith Pachiarz, Ph.D., St.
Louis U.
1972 Gerilee Gustason, Ph.D., U. of
So. Calif.
1975 Inge Goldstein, Ph.D.,
Columbia U.
1975 Teena Wax, Ph.D., U.
of Delaware
1976 Betty G. Miller, Ed.D., Penn
State U.
1976 Lucille Vida Miller, Ph.D.,
Brigham Young U.
1978 Nancy E. Kensicki, D.A.,
Catholic U.
1979 Barbara Bauer, Ph.D., N.Y.U.
1979 Susan Feder, M.D., Emory U.
School of Med.
1980 Sheila Conlon, J.D.,
Georgetown Law Center

1980 Judith L. Johnson, Ed.D.,
Gallaudet U.
1980 Jane Reehl Dillehay, Ph.D.,
Carnegie Mellon U.
1980 Roslyn Goodstein Rosen,
Ed.D., Catholic U.
1980 Mary Jane Sweeney Moore,
J.D., Catholic U.
1982 Barbara Rae Lee, Ph.D., U.
of Michigan
1983 Barbara Boyd, Ph.D., U. of
So. Calif.
1983 Carol Padden, Ph.D., U.C.
San Diego
1985 Barbara Kannapell, Ph.D.,
Catholic U.
1986 Jane Kelleher, Ph.D., U.
of Iowa
1986 Irene W. Leigh, Ph.D., N.Y.U.
1987 Jan Lou Jones, J.D., U.S.C.
School of Law

1987 Linda (Risser) Lytle, Ph.D.,
Catholic U.
1987 Deborah Meranski
Sonnenstrahl, Ph.D., N.Y.U.
1988 Donalda Kay Ammons, Ph.D.,
U. of Maryland
1988 Mary Claveau Malzkuhn,
Ph.D., U. of Maryland
1989 Gertrude Scott Galloway,
Ph.D., Gallaudet U. (ABD)
1989 Betty Bounds-Wood, Ed.D.,
Oregon State U. (ABD)
1989 Sharon Heidyt Carter, Ph.D.,
Brigham Young U. (ABD)

Honorary Doctorates

Bestowed by Gallaudet

Helen Northrup	1956
Petra Howard	1960
Regina O. Hughes	1967
Edna P. Adler	1980
Marlee Matlin	1987

At Gallaudet University & Pre-College Programs

There are several funds in the name of deaf women at Gallaudet University: The Agatha Tiegel Hanson Service Award; Belle Merrill Draper Fund; Alan and Florence Crammatte Fellowship Fund; James and Doris Orman Fellowship Fund; and Catherine Bronson Higgins PKZ Scholarship Fund.

Gerilee Gustason. Courtesy of Gallaudet Archives.

Gerilee Gustason was the first deaf woman president of the Convention of American Instructors of the Deaf (CAID). Her term was 1983-85. She is co-author of *"Signing Exact English."*

Mary Claveau Malzkuhn, a Gallaudet University professor, was chosen by the Student Body Government for the Teacher-of-the-Year Award in May 1986. She attended the Michigan School for the Deaf at Flint and went to Gallaudet many years later after raising three sons.

Mary Ann Pugin, from Indiana,

Mary Ann "MAP" Pugin. Gallaudet Photo Lab.

is the first Director of Gallaudet University Alumni House on campus. It is known as "Ole Jim."

Nancy Jones Lewis, of California, conducted more than 50 deafness-related workshops in New Zealand and Australia before her husband joined her to tour Asia in 1986. Both are with Gallaudet University.

Georgette Duval Fleischman, of Florida, was honored as Volunteer-of-the-Year in 1986 for her excellence in interpreting

Agnes Minor Padden

for French-speaking visitors at Gallaudet University.

Agnes Minor Padden, a graduate of Kendall School in Washington, D.C., was the first, full-time, deaf female Physical Education instructor at Gallaudet College. After several years of absence to raise two children, she returned and has taught English at Gallaudet since 1953.

Daisy Slagle Cartwright of California, Peace Corps Volunteer, served in Nepal.

Left to right: Nancy E. Kensicki receiving an award from Dr. Lee, former president, and Dr. King Jordan, president of Gallaudet University.

Nancy Evans Kensicki, the first deaf woman to hold a doctorate in English, is also the first deaf person in the history of Gallaudet University to chair the English Department, one of the largest departments on campus. She is the editor of the Journal, *Teaching English to Deaf and Second-Language Students.* She was the 1987 recipient of the Second Annual President's Distinguished Faculty Award.

The Graduate Fellowship Fund (GFF) Committee at Gallaudet, chaired by Nancy in 1965, awarded $34,600 to 10 deaf doctoral students for the 1987–88 academic year.

Seven of this year's recipients are deaf women: Carolyn Stern, studying medicine at Northwestern University Medical School; Kathleen Samuel, studying clinical psychology at the California School of Professional Psychology; Bonnie Ryan, studying law at the Columbus School of Law in Sacramento, Calif., Laurie Lee Johnson, studying psychology/clinical psychology at the Univer-

sity of Minnesota; Teresa Curtin, studying law at New York University School of Law; and Karen Lee Christie, studying special education at the University of Pittsburgh.

Ausma Smits, a native of Latvia and Gerilee Gustason were two of the three founders of the Deafness Related Concerns Council, now the President's Council on Deafness at Gallaudet University. Under Ausma's leadership, four studies covering in-house issues were completed and

Ausma Smits

presented to the administration: Interpreting, Telecommunication Devices, Orientation to Deafness and Deaf People and Employment of Deaf.

Several deaf women have chaired Gallaudet University departments since 1974. First was Ausma Smits who headed the History Department for ten years. Others have included Edith Rikuris (Biology), Gerilee Gustason (Education), and Betty G. Miller served as acting chairwoman for one semester (Art).

Nancy Bloch, a nine-year employee of the University, is director of the School of Management's Management Institute. The management institute is a first ever specifically designed for deaf professionals in this country.

Marianne Sassen. Gallaudet Photo Lab.

At Pre-College Program, Marianne Sassen from Missouri, became the first deaf woman Program Supervisor at the KDES Intermediate and Middle School departments. And at MSSD, Cynthia Neese Bailes from Georgia is the new principal.

Faculty at the Pennsylvania Institution for the Deaf and Dumb (Mt. Airy), ca 1890. Courtesy of Gallaudet Archives.

Entertainment

Dance

In the year of 1920, wrote **Mrs. George T. Sanders** in *The Silent Worker,* dancer **Cecile Hunter** taught dancing near Cornell University with great success for some years. She also taught the art in New York City as a side occupation. In the 1920's, **Mobi Urbanocs** was a renowned deaf dancer in Europe. She was a pupil of **Stephanie Klumesova**, ballet mistress of the National Theatre in Prague, Czechoslovakia.

During the mid-1920's, **Helen Elizabeth Heckman** (b. 1898) of Muskogee, Oklahoma impressed audiences in small European night clubs with her dancing. She was

Previous Page. Gallaudet Photo Lab.

once awarded second place in a national contest of Beauty of Face and Figure. She authored *My Life Transformed* in 1928. She became deaf at the age of eleven months and was not stimulated until she was 12 years old. Helen owed the success to her stepmother who taught her to enunciate, sing and dance. She performed before the Congressional Club in Washington, D.C. and many other places during the 1920's.

Frances Woods (nee Esther Thomas) was born deaf but learned to dance by feeling the rhythm of the music. She met her hearing husband on a dance floor in Ohio and as a team they traveled all over the country in the 1930's–1950's. There is a likeness

of Frances Woods, the Wonder Deaf Dancer, in one of the "Believe It or Not" museums.

During her retirement years, Frances gave lessons to senior citizens and handicapped people to uplift their spirits.

Virginia Downey, who attended the Lexington School circa 1939–1940 became a chorus girl in a couple of Broadway shows. She was also pictured on the cover of the *Police Gazette* which is probably why she was invited to leave Lexington. Virginia toured with some vaudeville acts and a Gallaudet student, schoolmate of Virginia's, visited her backstage at the RKO Keith in Washington, D.C.

The Colonial Days Minuet — Circa 1900.

Florita Corey

Florita (Flo) Tellez Corey was the first deaf professional Spanish and Mexican dancer. She specialized in the South American, Tango, Rhumba, and Conga during the 1930's and 40's. Flo studied at the Cusick Dancing School in Tuscon, Arizona, where she met her dancing partner Jose Cota.

During World War II, Flo and Jose teamed up for USO tours, which entertained over 20,000 people and were responsible for the sale of over one million dollars in war bonds. Flo now resides in Oakland, California, with her husband Charles. Her daughter, Rita, is an assistant professor at Gallaudet Theatre Arts.

After three years as an actress with NTD, **Rita Corey** went on to become a dancer and the COREY-ograph director for MUSIGN, a sign language, mime, dance group based in Berkeley, California, from 1980 to 1986. She was also the understudy to Freda Norman as

Sarah in the National Touring Company of *Children of a Lesser God* during 1982. Rita gave dance instruction to a group of youngsters from the Luther Burbank School who participated in "The Event of the Year" with Whoopie Goldberg. Many schools have recently begun implementing Rita's Visual Art workshop in their curriculum (mime, dance, signing, song, drama, and music video).

Fannie Yeh, an emigrant from Taiwan at the age of 14, taught creative dance (the fine points of body movement), drama and puppetry at various schools and NAD's Pageantry. When she moved to Hawaii in the 1970's, Fanny obtained a grant from the National Endowment of the Arts for the creative dance workshops. She is a cofounder of the National Deaf Dance Theatre and is the Marketing Director for Information and Communication Systems, Inc., in Frederick, Maryland.

Yola Rozynek, a renowned deaf professional dancer from Israel, was trained at the Bat-Dor Ballet School and Bat-Yam Institute for the Arts. She taught at the National Theatre of the Deaf's Professional Theatre School in the summer of 1985. Currently she is a choreographer at MSSD.

Music

Evelyn Glennie is a deaf musician who graduated from the Royal Conservatory of Music in England in 1986.

At the age of three, **Beryle Kalin** started singing with her sisters at church functions. After a bout with the measles, she lost most of her hearing when she was four. In 1987, at the age of 84, she continued her singing and was with

the New Orleans Opera Chorus.

Maryland's **Julie Bartee** worked with country singer Loretta Lynn in 1971, and again in 1985 for the United Way Fund Drive on TV. From time to time Loretta and Julie have exchanged greeting cards.

World-famed opera diva, soprano Beverly Sills, arranged to have some opera performances captioned for her hearing-impaired daughter, "Muffy" **Meredith Greenough**, as well as for hearing-impaired opera lovers. The captions, in English, were flashed above the proscenium.

Estella Bustamante, Stephanie Gemmill, Donna McGee and two male students rendered the National Anthem in sign language at the October 18, 1986, Washington Redskins football game in Robert F. Kennedy Stadium.

Stage

Deaf theatre gives the deaf community a way to appreciate and enjoy modern drama and comedy. A film with **Mary Williamson** reciting Longfellow's poem, *The Death of Minnehaha* in ASL is probably the oldest existing film of a deaf woman performer. It was made in the 1920's before TV days. When silent movies became sound movies in 1927 and screened captions disappeared, the deaf could not as easily enjoy public cinema.

Sign-mime involves using theatrical gestures, ASL signs and that other form of visual communication called body language. It uses very little fingerspelling which is difficult to read at a distance.

Imaginative directors and skilled actors combine ASL and pantomime to make deaf theatre richly expressive. The props and scenery are usually simple; movement is

Left to right: Sue Gill-Gould, Rita Corey and Fanny Yeh formed the National Deaf Dance Theatre. They sign, "This is the time to do it right now."

It was an exciting experience and many students tagged along to New York with the troupe. One of them was **Kathleen "Kit" Bedard** (Schreiber) who can still remember her most memorable and embarrassing moment there.

She writes:

"My date invited me, the naive Minnesotan, to attend the play in New York and after the play was over we went backstage to congratulate the actors and actresses on their superb performances. On

Below: Hazel Pike and Sam Stakley of Akron, Ohio, as a husband-wife team. Photo Credit: Picture Gallery.

Bottom: Jollity Club at Gallaudet, ca 1915.

planned so signs are easy to see.

Through the ages, gestures and mime have been important parts of the theatre. In recent years many deaf groups have evolved from producing deaf club skits to full-blown theatrical presentations. The National Theatre of the Deaf (NTD) is perhaps best known for what it calls sign-mime.

The women students at National Deaf-Mute College were asked to sit back with a male chaperone while men were seated in the front viewing an all-male cast play. During those days, it was not encouraging for women to form a club. That led them to found a literary club named Jollity Club in 1892. Until 1926 the coeds formed the Saturday Night Dramatics Club.

It was not until 1940 that Gallaudet offered formal dramatics courses. Many coeds who trained under the direction of Professor Frederick Hughes later joined the National Theatre of the Deaf.

Audree Bennett Norton was one of his proteges.

In the early 1940s, Boris Karloff was the star of *Arsenic and Old Lace* on Broadway. Eric Malzkuhn played the same role in the same play at Gallaudet College directed by Professor Frederick Hughes.

Deaf actresses in it were **Julia Burg, Frances Lupo** and **Arlene Stecker**. The company in New York City invited the Gallaudet group to perform one show in its Broadway theatre in 1942.

stage, actor Karloff was a strong, sinister performer. Off stage he gave one the impression of a shy humble person.

"He asked me if I would like to have his autograph. I answered — without thinking, 'What for! I collected stamps, not autographs.'

"Suddenly the tableau of characters before me seemed to freeze into a single frame—the shocked, shamed look of my escort, and the stunned and almost hurt look of the actor, and the accusing look and polite smiles on the faces of the other actors all hit home at once and I longed to disappear into a hole into the floor.

"My cheeks were burning long after we left the theatre and I do not recall how we excused ourselves from my faux pas."

Ana McGann, of Illinois, was known for her beautiful, artistic rendition of The Star Spangled Banner during the early years of this century. Ola Benoit Brown had this honor in the '30s, followed by Susie Koehn Ayers in the '40s.

Myrtle Allen of Minnesota, was known during the past three decades for her gracious rendition of Auld Lang Syne at various conventions.

Virginia Dries, Evelyn Zola, Celia Burg Warshawksy, Lil Andrewjeski and Deborah Sonnenstrahl, to name a few, were instrumental in starting several local theatrical groups. They gave performances at local clubs for the deaf and at state and national conventions from the 1930's to the 1970's.

Virginia's Freda Norman had the lead role of Sarah in Children of a Lesser God with the second national touring company. She is also known as Supersign in the children's TV series Rainbow's

End, who comes to the rescue of those having communication problems.

The spring of 1987 found Freda playing the leading role in The Good Person of Szechuan in Berkeley, California. The production's cast of 24 included blacks, Asian-Americans, an American Indian and Freda as a deaf performer.

As Dolly Levi in The Matchmaker, Freda was a hit on the stage at NTID in the fall of 1987. The comedy by Thornton Wilder

Freda Norman as SuperSign (Penny) in Rainbow's End. Photo Credit: D.E.A.F. Media, Inc.

was the basis for the musical Hello Dolly.

Johnny Belinda, a play about an illiterate deaf woman falling in love with the town physician was a hit show on New York's Great White Way in 1941. Florence Lewis May, a curator at the Hispanic Society of America in New York City, coached the actors' sign language. The director was so fascinated by her that he offered her the leading role. Florence declined as she was committed to a project in Spain at that time.

Julianna Fjeld starred in the 1987 production of Tennessee Williams' The Glass Menagerie directed by Don Bangs. It was sponsored by the University of California's Department of Dramatic Art. The troupe traveled and performed in several cities in California.

In 1980, Tales From A Clubroom, a play by Bernard Bragg and Eugene Bergman, was a hit at the NAD Centennial Convention in Cincinnati. Eileen Bechara, Lilly Berke, Georgette Doran, Adele Shuart, Nancy Torbett, Libby Hathaway and Sarah Val were the actresses in this play.

Women Talk, a one-act play by Bruce Hlibok, is about two deaf women comparing their lives: one is married to a deaf man and the other to a hearing man. In the original cast were Ellen Roth of New York and Linda Herenchak of New Jersey.

Judy Ann Diot, a graduate of the Washington State School for the Deaf, received a bachelor degree in Elementary Education and Dance from Western Oregon State College in 1981. She taught mime courses to undergraduate students there.

Judy Diot (left) in a play presented at Gallaudet.

She was nominated by a panel of judges at Western Oregon for the Best Actress Award for her performance in *West Side Story.* In another performance in *Dollhouse,* she was the deaf aunt and the hearing cast signed to her on the stage.

Judy currently works in the Special Opportunity Program at Kendall Demonstration Elementary School. **Jacqueline Seeburg Kilpatrick**, of Washington State, after training with NTD, assisted her husband actor Brian at the Fairmont Theatre for the Deaf in Cleveland, Ohio. She had the leading role in *Beauty and the Beast,* a PBS-TV Production in 1978. Now she is with a community theatre in Houston, Texas.

Detroit Sign Company — Deaf Theatre was fortunate to have **Rose Mantz** as a consultant for many years. The group honored her for her work promoting deaf awareness in the 1980's.

Carol Billone of the Marlton School for the Deaf, Los Angeles, and **Bette Darlene Hicks** of the Maryland School for the Deaf, Frederick, are known for their *Wow Them* high school drama productions.

Three of Carol's seven high musical shows at Marlton School, between 1971-77, received Los Angeles Mayor's Awards.

Carole Addabbo, an actress with the NTD, was the only deaf person to perform in the Edinburgh Theatre Festival in Scotland in 1986. She joined the Spectrum Deaf Theatre (Texas) for a number of years in the late 1970's.

Hedy Udkovich Stern, while at Gallaudet in 1973, played the role of Alice in Gilbert Eastman's original production of *Sign Me Alice.* Years later, she and **Julianna Fjeld** directed a cast of 28 in the California School for the Deaf, Fremont, 1987 high school play *Sign Me Alice.*

Dorothy "Dot" May Squire Miles, born and educated in the British Isles, made an important contribution to the stage. Her scripts involved deaf people in common, everyday situations. She polished her talents as an actress and playwright at the NTD.

One of her works, *A Play of Our Own,* based on deaf experiences was adapted from the 1967 movie, *Guess Who's Coming to Dinner.* The drama deals with the mixed marriage between a deaf woman and a hearing man.

Her 1975 thesis, *"The History of Theatre Activities in the Deaf Community of the U.S.,"* has never been published. *"Don't sit back and dream about it,"* was her motto. *"Do something about it!"*

Dorothy "Dot" Miles

Elizabeth "Liz" Quinn, a Connecticut Yankee, has been portraying a deaf character on the stage in England. Earlier when with Spectrum Deaf Theatre in Texas from 1977 to 1980, she played a leading role in *The Blue Angel* adapted and directed by J. Charlie McKinney.

Liz directed *Beauty and the Beast* for PBS TV in 1978 utilizing local deaf talent and elementary students of the Texas School.

Sharon Wood as the Beast

Sharon Wood portrayed the Beast in this production and Sandi Inches-Vasnick, now with NTD, was the beauty.

While residing in England in 1984, she co-authored, *Listen to*

Phyllis Frelich as Janice in **Love is Never Silent.** **Photo Credit: Gallaudet Today.**

Me: The Story of Elizabeth Quinn.

Michelle Banks received a prize for her performance as Titania in Shakespeare's *A Midsummer Night's Dream* and her role as *Miss Brown* in the Broadway show *For Colored Girls.* She is a former KDES and MSSD student now attending Gallaudet.

Phyllis Frelich, the eldest daughter of a North Dakota deaf family with nine children, won the 1980 Tony Award for Best Actress in the Broadway hit, *Children of a Lesser God.*

In The Hands of Its Enemy is the second play Mark Medoff wrote for Phyllis. This one focuses on a deaf playwright, Marietta Terby.

It was during the play *Iphigenia in Aulis* when David Hays spotted Phyllis performing at Gallaudet and he invited her to the O'Neill Center Theatre summer school in 1966.

"Fortunately David Hays formed NTD the same year I was graduated from Gallaudet in 1967,"

says Phyllis. *"He invited me to be one of the founding members. The rest is history."*

Phyllis portrayed a deaf prostitute in *Barney Miller,* an NBC-TV show, in 1981; and a lonely heart columnist writer in ABC's *Spencer For Hire* in 1986.

Phyllis and Bonnie Tucker, a lawyer, were interviewed by Ted Koppell on *ABC Nightline.* The occasion was held during the February 1987 inauguration of closed-captions on the national network TV news series.

Mary Beth Miller

Mary Beth Miller, a native of Louisville, Kentucky and an adopted daughter of New York City, is a comedienne and dramatic actress who helped found the New York Deaf Theatre. After several years with the National Theatre of the Deaf, she wrote and directed several plays. Among her credits are *A Play of 1,000 Words* and *ASL Festival* which focused on experiences of deaf individuals.

"My experience as one of the NTD members," says Mary Beth, *"has helped me see how lucky I am to be living in America. Deaf people in the (rest of) the world are not as fortunate as Deaf Americans are and NTD has helped me explore the abilities I have."*

She taught sign language to William Hurt for his leading role in the film production of *Children of a Lessor God.*

With Remy Charlip and George Ancona, Mary Beth published *Handtalk. An ABC of Fingerspelling, Sign Language and Handtalk: Birthday.* She is currently developing videotapes in sign language about famous deaf people.

Susan Jackson, a product of the Illinois School for the Deaf in Jacksonville, is a veteran performer. She was with Hughes Memorial Theatre (Washington, D.C., 1968–1981), before joining NTD (1982–1986). She went abroad in England to play the role of Doris in *Equus* for six months. Susan won both Most Versatile

Story teller, Susan Jackson.

Performer and Most Promising Actress Awards for her acting in *Anastasia* directed by Betty Miller.

Several former MSSD students under tutelage of Eric Malzkuhn and Tim McCarty have been in show business:

Terrylene's play, *Imagine,* was produced at the Kingshead Theatre in London, England. She, a descendant of many generations of deaf relatives, was featured in the role of a deaf, street-wise teenager in one of the *Cagney and Lacey* TV programs in 1987. She also portrayed a witness to murder in an episode of *Beauty and the Beast* on CBS in 1987.

Cheryl Jaglowski-Lundquist and Charity Reedy performed in *Children of a Lesser God,* a joint effort fo the University of Maryland and Gallaudet University in Fall of 1987 and Spring 1988. The cast was an experimental mixture of students from both universities. Mary Ellen Martone was the co-producer of this play. Monique Holt has been cast as Kate in New York University's production of *Taming of the Shrew.*

Children of a Lesser God

While in New Mexico, Phyllis Frelich and her hearing husband Robert Steinberg, helped writer/director Mark Medoff with the story of *Children of a Lesser God* by providing details of the deaf culture.

Phyllis opened the door to other deaf performing artists by winning the 1980 Tony award for her excellent performance in *Children* on Broadway.

The Hallmark Hall of Fame TV production of *Love Is Never Silent* was based on the novel, *In This Sign,* by Joanne Greenberg. Phyllis

portrayed a deaf mother in the 1930's. *Love Is Never Silent* is the story of two deaf parents dependent on their hearing daughter for contact with the hearing society.

Phyllis signed a 13-week contract to portray Sister Sarah, a mysterious nun in NBC's daytime soap opera, *Santa Barbara,* in the fall of 1988. She teamed for the first time with Marlee Matlin in a two-hour CBS movie, *Bridge to Silence.* It is about a deaf widow who had to fight her own parents for the custody of her hearing child.

In England and Australia, Elizabeth Quinn played the role of Sarah in *Children of a Lesser God.* *"It is also important that deaf children have parts in the play. I think role models for young deaf students are a relevant consideration in deaf children's theatre. Too often, these children think of themselves as incapable of being performers."* Elizabath captured Britain's top award, the Society of West End's 1983 Theatre Actress of the Year, for playing the role of Sarah in *Children of a Lesser God.* She was the first performer to win such an award.

Julianna Gold had a supporting role as Lydia in the original play, along with Phyllis Frelich.

Actress Marlee Matlin, of Illinois, won the Golden Globe Award for Best Dramatic Actress in January, 1987. She played Sarah in the movie *Children of a Lesser God.* She later won the 1987 Oscar Award for Best Actress.

The same year she was awarded an honorary Doctor of Humane Letters degree from Gallaudet University in May, and a month later, an honorary Doctor of Fine Arts degree from Marymount Manhattan College in New York.

Marlee Matlin. Gallaudet Photo Lab.

Marlee spent three days swimming in the water rehearsing the pool scenes with William Hurt for the movie production of *Children*.

"I'm an actress who just doesn't happen to hear," smiles Marlee. *"I have my own hearing, you see. It's different from your hearing, but it's my own."*

In August, 1987, Marlee was named one of the 18 most beautiful women in America by fashion magazine *Harper's Bazaar.* She was featured on the cover with Rob Lowe in the March/April issue of *In Fashions.*

She was the honored Presenter of the Best Actor Award at the 1988 Oscar Award Ceremonies.

During the "Deaf President Now" demonstrations at Gallaudet University, Marlee appeared on Ted Koppel's *ABC Nightline* show with Greg Hlibok and Elisabeth Zinser. Marlee's comment, *"I think the Board of Trustees are deaf inside; 124 years of one-way com-* munication is too much,"* was quoted extensively.

She was among 10 people who received 1988's Jefferson Awards for public service by the American Institute for Public Service at an annual ceremony held in the Supreme Court building.

Allison Gompf was featured in *Children* as Lydia, the lead singer. Later she won a scholarship from the Presidential Scholars Program. She did the interpretation of monologues from *A Midsummer Night's Dream* and from *Sweet Aloes* in Washington, D.C.

Lenore Helberg, a legally deaf-blind student, took the role of Sarah in *Children* at Ohlone College in Fremont, California. She received a standing ovation.

Ella Mae Lentz got the leading role of Sarah in Chicago, **Leitha Summerlin** in Indianapolis; **Maureen O'Grady** in San Diego and **Bobbie Beth Scroggins** in Dallas. There have been many others.

Yola Rozynek starred in the leading role of Sarah in the Israeli production of *Children*.

Television

Deaf Mosaic, the nationally broadcasted program for and about hearing-impaired people, is a production of Gallaudet University's Department of TV, Film and Photography. *Deaf Mosaic* is now available in more than 30 million homes. It is presented three times a week on the cable television and on PBS's affiliated stations throughout the United States, Canada and Japan. The program is jointly produced by a staff of deaf and hearing television professionals.

Jane Norman, Mary Lou Novitsky and Rachel Stone-Harris were the original regular rotating hostesses along with the host, Gil Eastman.

Mary Lou Novitsky, an associate producer, arranges monthly shows which include highlights of the lives and activities of deaf people. In 1987, for the second consecutive year, *Deaf Mosaic* received two Emmy awards as the outstanding independent production from the Washington Chapter of the National Academy of Television Arts and Sciences. The 1987 Emmys were given in recognition of the individual achievement of the program hosts, Gil Eastman and Mary Lou Novitsky.

Toby Rae Silver has a BA degree from the University of Maryland and an MA degree from the University of Texas. She was the first deaf woman to major in Radio/Television/Film. Toby works as a freelance TV and Cable TV producer-director, chiefly in the metropolitan Washington, D.C. area.

Toby and Mary Lou Novitsky of ML Silver Production have produced some major video works including *Signing Naturally:*

Mary Lou Novitsky. Gallaudet Photo Lab.

The Vista American Sign Language Student Videotext for DawnSignPress in 1988 and in 1987, *A Celebration of Deaf Women's Culture,* sponsored by the Deaf Women United Conference Committee and Roadwork, in celebration of International Women's Day.

Jane Norman started *Newsign 4* on KRON, a first in the San Francisco area with deaf newscasters on a daily program. She and Peter Wolf presented a summary of current news along with special items of interest to the deaf audience.

The program won an Emmy award in the 1970s and it was the inspiration for several other deaf people in America to become TV newscasters. **Joyce McCallon Lynch** replaced Jane Norman and Peter Wolf after a few years.

Jane was selected as one of the subjects in *Profiles in the Arts* published in 1986 by the National Endowment for the Arts and the President's Committee on Employment of the Handicapped. Her favorite quotation is, *"An artist is someone who communicates what he or she believes in and feels most deeply."*

Washington, D.C.'s first deaf anchorperson, **Cynthia Saltzman,** did a morning news program signing and moving her lips while the voice speaker read during the news on T.V. in 1972. The TV station personnel requested that Cynthia announce the warnings for deaf people during storms. Cynthia said, *"This is like a dream life for me. I spent all of my childhood trying to help my deaf sister. Now I can help thousands of deaf people every day."*

Mary Beth Barber, Miss Deaf America 1980, was a guest star on *MacGyver.* She helped him to expose an international weapons dealer. Richard Dean Anderson, who is MacGyver on the show, awarded Mary Beth with a bouquet of flowers after the taping of the show.

Mary Beth was the director of the 1987 Miss CAD Pageant in Santa Clara, California. She is currently with the *Silent Festival* in Los Angeles.

Beth Ann Bull, child actress and model for the John Tracy Clinic, was the actress featured in McDonald's *Silent Persuasion*

Beth Ann Bull

TV commercial in 1987 and 1988. She was graduated from NTID in Rochester, New York.

Sheila Lenham had a part with Sonny Bono on the *Love Boat.*

Mary Vreeland appeared in *Have You Tried Talking to Patty?* which was an after-school CBS special in January 1986.

Stephanice Beacham (Sable Colby in *The Colbys* and *Dynasty*) has hearing problems but she has a very sexy British accent. She had planned to be a teacher of deaf children.

Most of the distaff side of the deaf world is glued to the tube every Wednesday night when ABC's *Dynasty* is televised.

Judy Pratt was a student at Gallaudet College when she was chosen to play in the PBS TV series, *The Voyage of the Mimi* in the early 1980's.

Nanette Fabray, TV comedienne/ actress, has given much of her time to the education of hearing loss.

Born Ruby Nanette Fabar in San Diego, she has had hearing problems since her childhood days and wears hearing aids.

Nanette took sign language classes and her close friends, Caroline and Herb Larson, were her favorite tutors. Nanette appeared on Carol Burnett's TV show in the late 1960's, performed in sign language. The result was a lot of mail from discomforted viewers.

Joanne Kovach Jauregui is the founder and director of COMMUNI-VISION, Inc. in Berkeley. Her shows on local cable TV, *Bayside for the Hearing-Impaired* are about deaf people.

Julianna Fjeld, the only child of

Jane Norman & Julianna Field with her Emmy Award. Gallaudet Photo Lab.

a U.S. Army Colonel, grew up attending several schools for the deaf. After graduation from Gallaudet she joined the National Theatre of the Deaf; she was involved with the International Visual Theater in Paris, France; and returned to the states and purchased the rights to *In This Sign* by Joanne Greenberg.

Julianna played the role of Susan Anton's masseuse in the TV feature *Golden Girls.*

For 10 years she tried to get Hollywood producers interested in the book and finally Hallmark and CBS agreed to back the production. As the co-producer of the TV feature movie, Love Is Never Silent (1986) based on Joanne Greenberg's book In This Sign, Julianna was the first deaf person to win an Emmy Award. The networks originally wanted two hearing performers to play the roles. But with Julianna's persistence, the network decided to cast deaf performers to lead roles for a prime-time production.

She closely watched the production and editing process and insisted that several scenes be retaken to assure proper use of sign language.

In the spring of 1988, Julianna directed an adaption of *The Miracle Worker* at the California School for the Deaf in Fremont. It was set in 1988 and characterized a deaf family's struggle to deal with a deaf-blind daughter.

Audree Bennett Norton, from Minnesota, was a pioneer in portraying deaf women in TV shows in the 1960-1970's. She demonstrated the use of many gadgets as used by the deaf community as well as many characteristics of deaf culture.

Audree had roles in several TV

Audree Bennett Norton in National Theatre of the Deaf's "Tales of Kansane," 1967–1968.

series including *Mannix, Streets of San Francisco, Family Affairs,* and *Man and the City.* She also appeared with Desi Arnaz, Jr. in an ABC Movie of the Week.

She did TV commercials for Lux Soap, Dr. Pepper, Kodak, S.F. Federal Bank and others.

Audree entertained as half of a popular song-and-dance team with Bernard Bragg. She did more commercials on TV after two years with NTD where she was best known for her leading roles in *The Tale of Kasane* and *Gianni Schicci.*

Linda Marie Bove, from a deaf family in New Jersey, was the first deaf person to appear in a daytime TV serial, *Search for Tomorrow* in 1973. Eventually she became a permanent member of the popular children's program *Sesame Street.*

Linda is featured in two books, *Sesame Street Sign Language Fun*

and *Sesame Street Sign Language ABC with Linda Bove.*

For a few episodes Linda was Fonzie's deaf girl friend on *Happy Days* TV show and she had a cameo part in the film, *Children of a Lesser God.* She was the understudy to Phyllis Frelich on Broadway and had the leading role in the first national tour.

"Long ago I felt like a pioneer but I hope the pioneer days are over now," Linda stated. *"The doors are just a little bit open for deaf people to work in TV."*

Hearing children in **Lily Page Corbett's** neighborhood several years ago thought she was a *"Bionic Woman"* because she wore a hearing aid. Children wondered if she could hear really far away.

Lily came to Virginia to be the staff consultant for the Council for the Deaf. She arranges training programs in deafness for the public agencies to help develop understanding and awareness of the needs and problems of deaf people.

Helen Menken, star of the Broadway stage, was probably the first to use sign language on television. On a special day at the 1939 New York World's Fair in Flushing, students from Lexington School, Fanwood (NYSD) and others were guests at the fair. The NYSD marching band and the NYSD Provisional Company performed for the fair goers. During the TV demonstration, Broadway stage stars Bert Lytel and Helen Menken were presented. Helen addressed the audience and the TV cameras in the sign language she learned from her deaf parents.

Linda Bove

Elizabeth "Liz" Quinn in Blue Angel. *Photo by Danny Schweers.*

Yola Rozynek as Sarah in Children of Lesser God *in Israel.*

Allison Sara Gompf

Terrylene

Bobbie Beth Scoggins

Cheryl Jaglowski-Lundquist

ENTERTAINMENT

Top: The coed play, Cyrano De Bergerac *at Gallaudet, 1939. Courtesy of Eric Malzkhun.*

Bottom: All-male cast at Ohio School for the Deaf Drama Club during the time women were not allowed to perform with men. Notice two actors disguised as women. Ca 1893. Courtesy of Gallaudet Archives.

Opposite, Top: All-female members of Jollity Club. Some women did men's roles. Ca 1910. Courtesy of Gallaudet Archives.

Opposite, Bottom: All-male cast play. Some actors donned as women at Gallaudet College. Ca 1910. Courtesy of Gallaudet Archives.

Feminists

FEMINISTS

Angeline A. Fuller Fischer (1841–1925) was a leader of the feminists among the American deaf in the 1880's. Her number one goal was for National Deaf-Mute College (now Gallaudet University) to admit deaf women or she would start a separate college for deaf women only.

Angeline began losing her hearing at 13 and apparently she found comfort in writing poetry about the beauty of nature and the sounds she once heard. Among her other activities, she was a fighter for women's rights; she began by writing letters to the editor of the *Deaf Mutes' Journal.*

Angie, from Omaha, Nebraska, attended the Illinois School at Jacksonville, Ill., but could not do much school work due to her vision problems. At times when her sight returned for short periods, she put down in writing many poems and articles from memory.

Angie directed attention toward the need for a college for women when she heard that the men's college had received government funds to build a new, stately gymnasium (now Ole Jim).

Sarcastically she writes, *"Neither the students of the National College nor any other deaf-mute school wherein signs are used to any considerable extent, need the exercise of a gymnasium because sign language is eminently a muscular exercise."*

It was reported that Angie Fuller wrote to the Deaf-Mute Journal, *". . . the girls should repay the students by refusing to marry such*

Angelina Fuller Fischer

students of a selfish, unchivalrous nature."

In the end, Miss Fuller pledged $5.00 to build a *"College for Mute Ladies"* or a *"Seminary for Deaf-Mute Girls"* to be situated as far removed from the men's college as possible.

Some $90.00 was contributed by the end of 1880, but public opinion had changed in favor of higher education for women and National Deaf-Mute College soon became coeducational.

Mattie A. Brown made a determined effort to enter Gallaudet College in 1879. It was said she left her home state before being graduated from the Minnesota School to fight the old argument of insufficient housing for women at the college.

Georgia Elliott, a senior at the Illinois School for the Deaf,

Previous page. Deaf President, NOW Activists at the rally–March 1, 1988. Gallaudet Photo Lab.

DEAF WOMEN

Top, Georgia Elliott (1886). Bottom, her hearing granddaughter, Catherine Kalbacher, currently a Professor at Gallaudet University.

appealed to the Convention of American Instructors of the Deaf in 1886 for a chance for deaf women to get a college education. It must have helped because the following year Gallaudet College opened the doors to co-eds. She enrolled the next year. Her hearing granddaughter now teaches Deaf Women Studies at Gallaudet University.

In the 1880's, deaf women were advised not to bring aprons to Gallaudet so they would not be laughed at.

Laura C. Sheridan, a self-appointed spokeswoman, according to reports, wrote a lengthy article *"The Higher Education of Deaf-Mute Women"* for the *American Annals of the Deaf*.

She used both logic and emotion to batter at the college's doors for deaf women. She felt they could not be expected to be as independent as hearing women and thus needed other and more established sisters to be their advocates. Sheridan wrote, *"the hope and ambition of entering college would raise still higher the general standard of deaf-mute intelligence."*

Harriet Martineau (1802–1972), a deafened English woman, was a militant intellectual during her time, an advocate for bettering the lives of all women. In her classic essay, *"Letter to the Deaf,"* she wrote; *"Be as wise as is possible under a great disability and as happy as is possible under a great privation."*

Laura Redden Searing (1840–1923) was a liberated deaf woman who wrote under the pseudonym *"Howard Glyndon."* [Glyndon, Minnesota, a small town near St. Paul was named in her honor.]

She graduated from the Missouri School for the Deaf and became a war correspondent during the Civil War where she saw men dying on the battlefields.

Laura interviewed President Lincoln and many Union generals with slate and chalk. Her war poems were published in 1864 and her *Belle Missouri* became the war song of the Missouri Unionists.

She authored the dedicatory poem in 1889 when the Gallaudet and Alice statue was unveiled on Kendall Green. In 1925, Florence Lewis, an alumna of the American School, recited the poem at the ceremony of the replica statue in Hartford, Connecticut.

Another of her poems was read at the dedication of deaf sculptor Douglas Tilden's *"Admission Day"* statue in San Francisco.

In 1985 one of the buildings on the Northwest Campus of Gallaudet University was dedicated and named in her honor: Laura Redden Searing.

Alice T. Terry grew up on a farm in Missouri and was educated at the state school for the deaf after several years of illnesses. She felt so sorry for her hearing siblings back on the farm as she was an avid reader and the books were not available back at home.

At age of 15 she decided to be a philosopher. After one year at Gallaudet with the Class of 1901, she entered a branch of Missouri State University.

Alice was the first female President of the California Association of the Deaf in 1923. At the tenth convention in Oakland in 1925, Alice was reelected.

During her tenure, the CAD went on record as supporting a bill to create a labor bureau for the deaf. This was passed by the Legislature but was ineffective because no funds were appropriated to run the bureau.

In 1927 the CAD successfully fought and defeated a bill that would have put the Berkeley School up for auction.

Laura Redden Searing

At a meeting during Alice Terry's reign as President of the CAD, her husband Howard lunged out from his chair to the platform and delivered himself thusly:

"I am not the President of the CAD nor Secretary nor any official but merely a plain member and listener extraordinaire. For breakfast my wife serves up to me fried CAD, for lunch I have boiled CAD, while at dinner time I feast on roast CAD. Then in the night when I am sick and weary of it all, the doctor making an erroneous diagnosis, prescribes that my wife shall cheer me up with an overdose of CAD. I tell you, fellows, life at home is just one darn CAD after another."

Having thus knocked the cover off the ball in the shortest speech of the evening, Howard sat down amidst thunderous applause from everyone except his wife.

Later on in the evening, coffee and cake were served and one of the fair charmers present remarked

Gallaudet Photo Lab. Gertrude Scott Galloway.

to Mr. Terry, *"This is CAD coffee and cake."* To which the Honorable Howard exclaimed, *"Well, I'll be d-----!"* (Or so it was claimed in the *The Silent Worker* of the time.)

After serving on the Board of Directors for several terms, **Gertrude Scott Galloway**, a product of Kendall School, was elected the first female President of the NAD during the Centennial year of 1980. She chaired the VII World Congress of the World Federation of the Deaf.

Culminating many years as an educator she became assistant Principal of the Maryland School for the Deaf in Columbia.

Gertie was the Vice-President of Gallaudet College Alumni Association in the 1970's and she served on the White House Conference Planning Advisory Board.

"We should have the right to work at equal pay, with equal opportunity if we want to and we should also have the right to choose not to," Mrs. Galloway stated. *"When we select a field, we should not be limited to traditionally female employment."*

"Marriage should be an option, not an assumed career that implies penalty if we don't 'make it'." she

concluded. *"If we want children, fine; if not, that's our right. 'Choice' is my favorite word."*

In 1986, she was one of eleven extremely qualified people appointed to serve on the National Commission on Education of the Deaf.

In October, 1987, Gertrude received the Agatha Tiegel Hanson award from Rosalyn Lee Gannon on behalf of the Laurent Clerc Cultural Fund Committee, *"In recognition of your roles as educator, consultant and leader of state, national and world organizations."*

The ceremony took place at the celebration of the first anniversary of Gallaudet's university status and the 100th anniversary of its admittance of female students. The big

event was chaired by Ausma Smits.

Susan B. Anthony Stewart, a direct descendant and a native of Buffalo, New York, was one of the speakers at the opening ceremony of the first Deaf Women Conference in Santa Monica, California in 1985.

The young, deaf Susan, majoring in Office Practice Procedures, graduated from NTID in 1974. She and her husband live in Detroit.

"I wish more deaf women had the opportunity to pursue advanced training," stated **Linda Risser Lytle**, a psychologist in the Washington, D.C. area. *"The reason it has taken me so long had more to do with lack of confidence than anything else. It may take us deaf women a bit longer to get where we want to be but don't underestimate us."*

Astrid Amann Goodstein at

Who Is A Real Woman?

*By English Department Students
Model Secondary School for
 the Deaf, Washington, D.C.*

"Amy Grant . . . for her great, hard work to spread Christianity."
—Gary Wolford

". . . fashionable, independent."
—Karl Ewan*

". . . has a positive attitude and smiles a lot."— Thao Cook

". . . can be anybody, a jogger, jailer, queen."— Marvin T. Miller*

". . . helpful, honest, loving, warm, caring."— Javire Torres

". . . doesn't have to prove she is equal because she knows she is."
—Abigail Finkle

". . . knows what she is doing and why she's doing it."— Diane Kubey*

". . . outspoken, productive."
—Ronal Shaffer

". . . enjoys a challenge, thinks positive."— Christopher Barbee

". . . will be there for children, husband."— Peggy St. John*

". . . against drugs."— Jill Crumley

". . . athletic, yet feminine, can marry and have children, yet be fashionable, famous."— Indrani Hewsen

". . . isn't afraid."— Beth Forman

". . . proud of self and children, responsible."— Wayne Mabry

". . . respects, accepts feelings, understanding of friends, enemies."— Tarhonda Sloan

". . . plays, wins, learns."— Lionel Simmons

". . . not afraid of love, not afraid of new things."— Darren Stokes

". . . very creative, encourages people to try their best."— Tammi Jerrett

". . . understands others' feelings, and me."— Darlene Ewan*

". . . loving in a warm, romantic way; loyal and kind to friends."
—Jeff W.

". . . cares for her body, full of life."
—Crystal Sullivan

". . . prepares for the future, makes successful decisions."— Darin Derkowski

". . . happy to listen to people, dignified and understanding."
—Matthew Lockhart*

". . . a really friendly person with lots of patience, loyalty and intelligence."— Stefan Bergan*

". . . livens up discussions, a good listener, not a show-off or gossiper."
—Raychelle Harris*

". . . not vain or a punk, although cool and in style."— Myra Yanke*

". . . my mother."— Joanne Russo

*children with deaf parent(s)

Gallaudet University adds, *"Deafness rather than the sex of a person was once the 'dead end' for the person seeking a doctoral degree."* Astrid co-authored the *"Interesting Deaf Americans — Reading and Writing Exercises,"* adopted from Helm's series of *"Interesting Deaf Americans."* She is an associate professor in the Department of English.

Patricia Hughes, from Virginia, a community outreach co-ordinator at the Community Service Center for the Deaf and Hard-of-Hearing in Seattle, was appointed to serve on the National Commission on Education of the Deaf in 1986.

She traveled all over the United States as a Section 504 Technical Assistance Trainer for the NAD in the early 1980's.

Patricia has won a Washington State award for her work in politics. She also chaired the state team on education of the deaf. The First California Regional Conference for Deaf Women invited Patricia as the keynote speaker.

"With the right attitude and some hard work, we can succeed in just about anything," asserted Virginia Tibbs. *"Remember that when one door closes, another opens,"* concluded the hearing-impaired author. *"It's up to you to look for those doors."*

"We deaf women always thought of ourselves as deaf people . . . our role as women was secondary," said **Christine Buchholz** of Los Angeles.

And for the menfolk, a little condescension: *". . . consequently, in order for change to occur not only should the woman get training, but so should the man . . . you know, Women's Lib means Men's Lib, too. . ."*

—Roslyn Goodstein Rosen,
Dean at Gallaudet

Nancy Bloom Rarus Shook has been an active member of the deaf community working at improving the quality of life for deaf citizens. A graduate of the New Jersey School, she had twice been elected to the Board of the NAD. While making her home in Arizona, she was the chairwoman of the Community Outreach Program of the Deaf Administrative Advisory Board. During that time she was appointed principal of the Junior High School Department at the Arizona School for the Deaf.

"I grew up somewhat confused as to which heritage I really belonged," writes **Donette Reins**, of Fremont, California. *"During my school days at the Idaho School in Gooding, I knew I was a little different from my peers in some ways because of my long braids, Indian clothes and especially my love for horses.*

"My deaf mother, a full-blooded American Indian, had never told us anything about our heritage. All my life I have been constantly exposed to deaf culture and womanhood.

"I am trying," she concluded, *"to instill some pride of our Indian ancestry into my three deaf children. I simply consider myself a deaf feminist first."*

"During one heated discussion at a student council meeting at the Maryland School when I was a student," writes **Sandra Ammons-Rasmus**, of Fremont, Calif. *"I stood up and made a 'protest' speech about the discussed issue: how frustrated many of the girls were about the many privileges the high school boys were getting whereas the high school girls did not. We felt the boys did not deserve many of them.*

"After I presented my brief 'protest' I sat down and just like a teenager would, sought some support from my counterparts. The student council sponsor interrupted with a smirk on his face saying, 'You all must think she is a woman libber! Ah, no! She is a woman lipper!' Then he joined the boys in the laughter.

". . . to this day," grumbled Sandra, *"I still can't laugh about it."*

Deaf Women

Everyday there's discrimination.
You see deaf women everywhere,
Fighting, arguing, signing
   viciously,
And all for the rights of deaf
   women,
Young and poor.
Even though competition is there
Day after day, deaf women want
To prove that they are equal,
Equal to the hearing people.
Sometimes employers will not
   employ,
Much less share any kind of
   information to deaf women.
But, listen here, I say, seriously.
We deaf women will collect
   equality
And we will go to the top,
To win what we deserve to get,
Recognition.
We may be deaf,
But we are humans, too!
We can love, we can cry.
We can do almost anything
   hearing women do.
We will win our rights,
Even if we suffer!
We're deaf women.
We request understanding from
   the hearing.

Written by Crystal Martin, Indiana School for the Deaf, age 15, 1988.

Literature

LITERATURE

Florance Lewis May

Self-educated author **Elizabeth Allen** wrote The *Silent Harp of Fugitive Poems* in 1832. It is possible that she was the first deaf poetess to be published.

Recollections of a Mute: A Brief Sketch of Events and Incidents Which Have Transpired With My Knowledge was written by **Miss A. R. Knight** in 1857. It was in the form of a small pamphlet (although the compound title took up most of the pages) *Harper's Magazine* in 1884, published *The Poetry of the Deaf* by Dr. E. M. Gallaudet. He named the better deaf poetesses of the time, including: Angie A. Fuller Fisher; Laura C. Redden Searing; Mary Toles Peet; and Laura Bridgeman. Later, Dr. E. A. Fay made a number of additions to that list and included Alice C. Jennings and Rachel J. Philbrick.

Out of Savannah, Georgia, came our first deaf novelist, **Rachel J. Philbrick,** who became deafened at the age of 12. Her poems and a number of romance novels were published before 1885.

Corrinne Rocheleau wrote *Heroic French Women of Canada,* in 1922. Although born south of the US-Canada border, she wrote in French, her native language.

Corrinne wrote several books portraying the Canadian background, English and French, providing a charming and interesting picture of life in the 1870's on a farm beside the St. Lawrence River.

Her books have special appeal; *Laurentian Heritage* is the best known of them.

Helen Heckman was probably the first deaf professional dancer. Her autobiography, *My Life Transformed,* was published in 1928.

Poetess **Alice McVan** was known and respected for her translations of Spanish lyrics. Her work appeared in the publication of the Hispanic Society in New York City. *Tryst* is considered her best and most impressive effort.

How to Be Happy Though Deaf was published in the *Catholic World* in 1935. In it, **Christine Whiting Parmenter** related her experiences with the bulky hearing devices of bygone days.

Florence Lewis May's 1939 book, the 417-page *Hispanic Lace and Lace Making,* is profusely illustrated with 432 of her drawings.

Loel Francis Scheiber was the editor-in-chief of *The Silent Worker* in the 1940s. **Muriel Strassler** became publications chief for the NAD in the 1980's. Her responsibilities encompassed The *Deaf American* and *The NAD Broadcaster.* Muriel now works for the University Center at Gallaudet.

Taylor Caldwell (1900–1985), a hearing-impaired and prolific author, has written over 50 novels; many were on the best-seller lists. In 1946, *Captains and the Kings* sold 4.5 million copies. Taylor said, *"I never had to rewrite; long years of effort left me permanently sober."*

Between 1948 and 1984, *The Silent Worker* and *The Deaf American* published 294 biographies of people important to the deaf community; among those who have left their mark were the women listed on the following page.

In the 1950's and 1960's **Geraldine Fail** of Long Beach, California and **Harriet Votaw** of Denver, Colorado, were the co-editors of *Swingin' 'Round the Nation* in The

THE SILENT WORKER — THE DEAF AMERICAN
Women Important to the Deaf Community

Queen Alexandria, April 4, 1970	Patsy Lynch, June 1, 1962
Sylvia Chapin Balis, March 1, 1951	Alice Jan McVan, February 2, 1984
Mary Beth Barber, January 1, 1977	Dorothy Squire Miles, July 7, 1977
June Becker, July 7, 1976	Jane Miller, February 2, 1974
Ann Billington, March 3, 1973	Jane Norman, April 4, 1973
Linda Bove, December 12, 1977	Frances "Peggy" Parsons,
Judith Rasmus Bravin,	October 10, 1975
January 1, 1982	Ruby Radar, January 1, 1977
Ruth Clarke, July 7, 1972	Michelle Craig Smithdas,
Nanette Fabray, January 1, 1983	December 12, 1976
Eleanor Sherman Font,	Debbie M. Sonnenstrahl,
November 11, 1976	October 10, 1977
Phyllis Frelich, December 12, 1980	Reatha Suttka, July 1, 1949
Jean Jansen, July 7, 1976	Alice T. Terry, November 1, 1950
Cheryl Kent, December 12, 1981	Celia Burg Warshasky,
Babette Krayeski, September 9, 1973	February 2, 1977
Juliette Gordon Low,	Cecile Willman, December 12, 1970
February 2, 1974	

Florence "Flo" Bridges Crammatte. Gallaudet Photo Lab.

Silent Worker. It was the favorite column of many readers.

A deaf Texan, **Hallea H. Stout,** wrote plays and composed songs in the 1960's. The best known of her works are *Silent Songs for the Silent* and *Thoughts in Poetry.*

"One comment made that I have never forgotten," wrote **Helen E. Muse** from Minnesota, a teacher at the Georgia School for the Deaf in Cave Spring, *"A deaf person could not write a book like that!' This was said about 'Green Pavilions.' At first, I resented it; then I began to think it was one of the highest compliments."* Her book was published in 1961.

She also authored and updated the history of Georgia School for the Deaf and it was published in the *Deaf American* in October, 1966. Later it was used in the

Rome News Tribune paper in part. The usage was added to one of the volumes: *History of Public Education in Georgia 1734–1976* by the State Board of Education.

She mentioned that the Georgia school has become known as the home of "straight language for the deaf" as a result of the pioneering of the late Edith M. Fitzgerald's key and method for teaching straight language to the deaf. The Fitzgerald Key has received international acclaim as a breakthrough in the difficult procedures of teaching the deaf the mechanics of sentence structure. Miss Fitzgerald taught there for a while in the 1930's.

Rhoda Clark, another advocate for a home for the aged deaf to be located in the San Francisco Bay Area, helped Gaylee Becker with her book, *Growing Old in Silence: Deaf People in Old Age.*

Florence Bridges Crammatte served as the first chairperson of the Gallaudet College Alumni's Laurent Clerc Cultural Fund Committee (1967–1973). She also chaired the fundraising campaign to restore the 19th century gymnasium (Ole Jim) for use as the Alumni House. As National president of Phi Kappa Zeta sorority (1960–1967) she established its biannual newsletter, *The Phi Kappa Zetan.* Upon retirement from the U.S. Department of Agriculture, as a statistical assistant, she continued to do volunteer work at the Alumni House and at the Mental Health Center for the Deaf in Maryland.

An expert in editing books, Florence has worked her magic on *Notable Deaf Persons, Proceedings of the 7th Congress of the* of the World Federation of the Deaf and *Deaf Persons in Professional Employment,* to name a few.

Notable Deaf Persons, by Guilbert C. Braddock (1975), edited by Florence, profiles 96 deaf personalities; deaf women included are: Mabel Hubbard Bell, Mary Boling, Alice Cogswell, Angeline A. Fuller Fischer, Sophia Fowler Gallaudet, Cornelia A. Lothrop, Maria M. Marois, Mary Toles Peet, Yvonne Pitrois, Princess Katherine Plantagenet of England, Laura Redden Searing and Mary E. Totten.

Biographies of Joan Tiller, Henna Berzinsh and Mary Barker Boyd are included in the 1979 study, Living with Deaf-Blindness.

"I had always dabbled around with poetry," commented **Kathleen "Kit" Schreiber,** *"but really started writing when my last girl went to Cal-State University, Northridge, to get her master's degree.*

"She had never been so far away from home, so I promised her a poem a week until she graduated," said Kit.

"I was then working toward my B.A. in English; we both finished in 1980. I had also promised to publish the poems, hence Dear Beth *was born.*

"When I visited with her in California, I found she had posted the poems all over her walls. She insisted they made wonderful wallpaper. From then on, every new one I sent was accompanied by a note, '. . . here is some more wallpaper'." Concluded Kathleen, *"we both agreed the next title will fit the subject and will be called 'Wallpaper'."*

Kathleen "Kit" Schreiber. Reprint from **Gallaudet Today.**

Great Deaf Americans, by John and Robert Panara has an excellent collection of 33 biographies — deaf women included are: Laura Redden Searing, Mabel Hubbard Bell, Julietter Gordon Low, Frances Woods, Phyllis Frelich, Linda Bove and Kitty O'Neill.

Jerry B. Crittenden reviewed the

three-volume *Gallaudet Encyclopedia of Deaf People and Deafness* for *Gallaudet Today* and complained that there was no special segment devoted to deaf women.

Contributors to the *Gallaudet College Encyclopedia of the Deaf People and Deafness* included: Edna Adler, Carol Garretson, Gerilee Gustason, Corrine Hilton, Barbara Kannapell, Nancy Kensicki, Ella Mae Lentz, Sheila Conlon Mentkowski, Marcella Meyer, Carol Padden, Ausma Smits and Deborah M. Sonnenstrahl.

Celia May Laramie Baldwin compiled Gallaudet Day Program Material. She has served on the Gallaudet University Alumni Association Board several terms. After teaching at the Utah School many years, she is now at the California School in Fremont.

Profiles of several better known black, deaf women were published in *Black and Deaf* in 1983. Featured were: Shirley Allen, Katie Brown, Mary Cheese, Lottie Crook and Sandi LaRue.

Buff and Blue Editors

May Martin (1868–1908) founded Gallaudet College students' newspaper, *Buff and Blue* in 1892. Because she felt uncomfortable attending business meetings, she let a male student be the editor-in-chief.

1909–10	Alice Nicholson
1927–28	Alice McVan
1935–36	Ruth Yeager (co-editor)
1943–44	Malvine Fischer
1953–54	Nancy Hutchinson
1954–55	Nancy Hutchinson
1956–57	Flora Clark
1958–59	Dorothy Miles
1960–61	Dorothy Miles
1967–68	Nancy Abbott
1970–71	Julie Munoz (co-editor)
1971–72	Linda Risser
1972–73	Kay Tuberg (co-editor)
1977–78	Bonnie K. Hughes
1978–79	Carlene D. Thumann
1979–80	Teresa Ezzell
1980–81	Tina Jo Breindel
1982–83	Minnie Mae Wilding
	Mary Keane
	Marta Belsky
1984–85	Sallie L. Jordan
1985–86	Laura K. Genrich
1988–89	Kathy Lorenzo

In preparation for the 1985 World Games for the Deaf in Los Angeles, a set of sports signs by Harley Hamilton and Nancy Kelly-Jones was published. Copies of translations (French, Italian, Japanese and other languages) were distributed free at W.G.D.

Lou Ann Walker, daughter of deaf parents, is the author of *Amy, The Story of a Deaf Child,* published in 1986. The book tells the life story of Amy Rowley, a deaf child whose case was carried to the U.S. Supreme Court. This case concerned interpreting services for Amy in the public schools. Miss Walker also authored *A Loss for Words.*

Kathie Lindenmayer Boltz of Cicero, Illinois, earned a Golden Poet-of-the-Year Award. She entered her poem *"You'll Never Know the Loneliness"* in the 1987 World of Poetry contest.

Her composition deals with deaf people struggling for understanding in the hearing world.

Mary Johnstone, born and raised in Pittsburgh, is a deafened senior writer and editor in the Publication and Production Department at Gallaudet University. She is editor of the *"People Plus"* section of *Gallaudet Today,* the University's quarterly magazine. While a second-year graduate student at Gallaudet, a job opened up as a writer for *ON THE GREEN,* the University's faculty and staff newsletter. She could not resist applying for it. *"I have been doing creative work all my life; that was*

Nanette Fabray and Mary Johnstone. Gallaudet Photo Lab.

my field; that was where my talents lay. In graduate school, I had begun to realize that I was trying to re-invent myself because of deafness; I was not comfortable. So when the chance for a writing career presented itself, I jumped at it. As things turned out, it was more than a job, it was another stage of education —tailor made for me. I love the work, and I have finally begun to write my own."

Frances "Peggy" Parsons, world traveler, total communication ambassador in the 1970's and 1980's, was an associate professor in the Art Department at Gallaudet University. Peggy published *Sound of the Stars,* a story of her experience on the island with her twin sister Hester (Pollai) Parsons Battad in Tahiti during the adolescent years. Peggy spent six weeks of the summer of 1986 traveling in the People's Republic of China. She

visited schools for deaf students and organizations of deaf people in 12 cities.

She authored *I Didn't Hear the Dragon Roar,* based on her solo journey through the heartland of China from Hong Kong to Kathmandu.

Frances "Peggy" Parsons

Hester (Pollai) Parsons Battad of California authored *Tahiti* and two more books, *Idioms for Deaf Children: Humorous Illustrated Idioms and Their Origins* and *Easy Illustrated Idioms and Proverbs for the Deaf.*

La Reine Lauritsen

La Reine Lauritsen, *Her Life and Work,* is a volume donated by her husband, Westley Lauritsen, to the Archives at Gallaudet.

La Reine has three children. The best known is Robert R. Lauritsen, the Program Director for Deaf Students at St. Paul Technical Vocational Institute.

Library

Edith M. Nelson (1890–1942), the second deaf librarian at Gallaudet College, directed the library and taught library science courses during the '30s and '40s. She ini-

tiated the Hall of Fame which enshrines former faculty members of Gallaudet and national leaders of the deaf. To date, Edith and Elizabeth Peet (deafened adult) are the only women so honored.

Edith, a Gallaudet graduate, taught at schools for the deaf before her appointment as librarian at Gallaudet in 1919. She also taught gymnastics, Latin, typing and business practice in addition to her library duties.

Helen Northrup was the first deaf librarian at Gallaudet from 1909 to 1919.

In 1980, **Alice Hagemeyer**, a District of Columbia Public Library employee for more than 30 years, created *The Red Notebook.* The book contains updated information on activities and issues that affect the deaf community. *"I wish that my parents were encouraged to get information about deaf people,"* she said. *"Information would have helped my parents and everyone understand all of the issues on deafness and deaf people's needs to communicate. With information, people can make good choices for themselves and the people that they love."* Her publications, *The Deaf Awareness Handbook for Public Librarians* and *The Public Library Talks to You,* are popular across

Alice Hagemeyer

the United States and in foreign countries.

Her duties as the staff consultant for the council are to develop training programs in deafness for the public and agencies to help develop awareness and understanding of the needs and problems of deaf people.

She was named the *Alumna of the Year* by the University of Maryland College for Library and Information Science Alumni Organization in 1987.

Metropolitan Washington Area Public Libraries celebrated the 200th anniversary of the birth of Thomas Hopkins Gallaudet during Deaf Heritage Week, December 6–12, 1987. Alice coordinated this big event; Sarah Val, Jackie Epstein, and Sharon Wood were three of the leading educators invited to speak at the festivities.

Irene Hodock

Irene Hodock of Indianapolis was the first secretary of the School for the Deaf Librarian Group (Assn. of Resource Personnel Serving the Hearing-Impaired). She has been with the Indiana School for nearly 40 years.

Marilyn Gustos is a librarian technician at the U.S. Geological Survey under the Department of the Interior. Her office in California holds a wealth of information on geology, earthquakes, and floods in the nation.

Marilyn Duncan McCallon is a Deaf Services Specialist at the San Francisco Public Library, Civic Center Main Branch. The library supports a co-operative library service for the deaf in the Bay Area.

Majoring in English at Purdue University, Virginia wrote her first novel called *The Palace of the Princess*. It is a mystery story about a young woman and her deafness. She chose the pen-name of Virginia Scott in memory of her baby son, Scott, who died. She is now a librarian in Washington State. *"Remember that when one door closes, another door opens. It's up to you to look for those doors,"* she kept on saying.

Dorothy (Kopecky) Simpson, at first taught deaf children at the California School for the Deaf, then preferred to be a deaf Librarian at the University of California Berkeley since 1952.

Marjorie Culbertson served for 10 years in the Descriptive Cataloging Division of the Library of Congress before her retirement in 1978.

She formerly worked as a librarian at the Virginia School for the Deaf and Blind, for the American Meteorological Society and then at the Federal Power Commission. She has written for a number of publications, including *The Deaf American*.

There is a bronze and glass display case at the Gallaudet University Library to display the works of deaf people. It was a gift in remembrance of Alice Jan McVan from co-workers at the Hispanic Society of America in New York City.

Corrine Hilton

Corrine Hilton, Archives Coordinator at Gallaudet University, arrived at Kendall Green in 1963. Today she is known as "the walking encyclopedia" of Gallaudet lore.

As a curator, she is responsible for over 30,000 photographs dating from 1842 to the present. Preservation techniques are her main concerns.

Medicine & Science

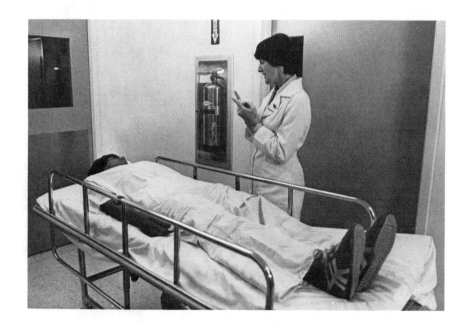

MEDICINE AND SCIENCE

May Paxton Benoit graduated from the Missouri School for the Deaf, Circa 1909. She was accepted as a student nurse. Her mentor was a female doctor who was one of the founders of the Children's Mercy Hospital in Kansas City, Missouri.

When May first came to the Children's Mercy Hospital, Dr. Katherine Richardson introduced her to Marian Finch of South Dakota, who later was hired as a nurse. They were led to the room they were to share. For the next two days, the women wrote notes to each other. After finding out that they were deaf signers from the other nurses, they burst into a big laughter.

Miss Lille "Bessie" Speaker of St. Joseph, Missouri, was hired later. The fourth one was Emma Brewington, who was in charge of the linen and worked in the nursery while the first three performed in the operation room.

Dr. Richardson wrote to May, *"For three years, you have been with us. It is wonderful that no man or woman or children to my knowledge made a complaint against you."*

She gave up her job to become Mrs. Benoit and the mother of three deaf daughters: Dora (Lamarie), Ola (Brown), and Ruth (Roberts). All of them were teachers of the deaf.

Alice Taylor Terry, a community leader in California, wrote in the November, 1923, issue of *The Silent Worker* about this unique experience: *"For my eye trouble, the doctor punched holes in my ears. . . nobody objected . . . I*

Previous Page. Jean Mulrooney. Gallaudet Photo Lab

remember distinctly the sharp needle, the process and the pain. But I did not cry; somebody had bribed me with a bright coin. Strangely enough, my eyes soon healed and have never bothered me since."

In the early 1950's, a nurse at the Ohio School encouraged Edna (Davies) Wilkinson and Mary Jo Schuer to try for careers in the field of medical laboratory technology.

After 21 years of experience working in a hospital in Pittsburgh and eight of those in the Cytology Department, Edna was appointed an Associate Professor at NTID in 1970.

Jean K. Cordano

Jean Kelsch Cordano is the Chief of Medical Technologists at Lakeland Hospital in Elkhorn, Wisconsin. She was granted a certificate in 1960 by the American Society of Clinical Pathologists.

"Deaf women," reports Jean, *"don't start planning for a job early enough."*

She explained that she "had" to take up the printing trade at the

North Dakota School because during the World War II years, the deaf boys were all working outside at local print shops.

During the summer months between college years, she was a linotype operator for the Mandan Daily Pioneer in Mandan (just across the river from Bismarck, North Dakota).

Following a year of teaching at the Wisconsin School for the Deaf, her interest in the medical field began when she worked with baby chicks on a poultry farm. She was a laboratory technician at Val-Lo-Will Farms, Lake Geneva, Wisconsin. Jean was honored with the *Alice Cogswell Award* from the Gallaudet University Alumni Association in the 1980's.

"We have come a long way. Ten years ago it was not quite 'OK' for a woman to assume all three roles—a worker, a mother and a homemaker. Today it is 'OK' with a notable change that a deaf woman now can take an active role in community service activities and/or organization work. We still have much to do," Jean quoted. (Reprinted from *"Women and Deafness," Gallaudet Today,* Summer 1984.)

The first deaf person ever registered by the American Society of Clinical Pathologists is Edith Goldston (Mrs. McKay) Vernon, who was a medical technician specializing in microbiology. A product of the Oklahoma School, her career took her to Texas and Maryland.

Frances Davis, a licensed practical nurse, was denied admission to the nursing program of a college in North Carolina. Her case was appealed to the U. S. Supreme

Court which concluded that *"Section 504 does not require colleges and universities [to] make substantial modification of standards [for the] handicapped."*

Jean A. Mulrooney from Ohio, a deafened nurse at Gallaudet, has conducted many workshops for deafened adult groups to reassure them that they can lead productive lives. Edna Shipley Conner and Joan Bartley, both deafened, do the same in the San Francisco Bay Area.

Nansie Sharpless

Nansie Sharpless (d. 1987), a deaf scientist at Albert Einstein College of Medicine in New York, had both M.D. and Ph.D. degrees. She specialized in brain research and was the chief of the Clinical Neuro-Psycho-Pharmacological Laboratory.

Her famed motto was, *"Use what you have and forget what you don't have. Why concentrate on what is missing?"*

Sharon Speck, who has a 70%

hearing loss and impaired vision, earned a bachelor's degree in nursing from Muskingum College/Case Western Reserve University in Ohio in 1961.

A year later after completing work in Salisbury, Rhodesia (now Zimbabwe) she was awarded her British Nursing Registration. She served as a staff nurse at the Muskingum College Health Center 1980–1984.

She assisted her husband in his successful campaigns for offices in the Ohio legislature.

Mary Jo Schuer has been employed at the Chillicothe Hospital in Chillicothe, Ohio for many years.

Martha Linstrom is a glassblower at a medical products glass company in Berkeley, California. She does the specific order tubes called "peanuts tubes" for hospital laboratories.

Susanne F. Dillman of Saginaw, Michigan, is currently employed as Medical Records Consultant/ Assistant to the Director of Medical Records at St. Mary's Hospital. Four area nursing homes are also the beneficiaries of her abilities in similar capacities.

As an active member of the Retinitis Pigmentosa Association, she has given talks to various groups and has been interviewed over the radio and local TV shows as part of fund-raising efforts to further research of Usher's Syndrome.

Julia Burg Mayes from New Jersey was honored for her many hours of volunteer work in the D.C. Metro area. Upon her retirement from the Michigan School and Model Secondary School for the Deaf, she earned a sapphire ring for contributing more than

four years of community service.

Her pet projects have been the Otis House, the halfway house in D. C., and the Visitors' Center at Gallaudet.

Julia has a new project — persuading local hospitals to provide TV caption decoders, TDDs and interpreting services for deaf patients.

"I would encourage other deaf women to do what I am doing," said Julia. *"I don't think deaf women realize the extent to which they are needed. There are many contributions they could make, especially older deaf women."*

Leslie Greer, an NTID graduate, was a histology technician at University Hospital in Stony Brook, New York. Her duties involve extreme skill and care while preparing microscopic slides for pathologists to study after biopsies have removed suspected cancerous or malignant growths from patients. Leslie, working with bodily tissues that contain possible deadly, transmittable diseases, must take exceptional care in preparing herself and her lab for the work. Absolute sterility of materials and equipment used and worn — gloves, masks, gowns, cap and shoe covers — is a necessity.

Irene W. Leigh, Ph.D., is a Clinical Psychologist, licensed to practice in New York State.

At the age of four in December, 1948, she and her hearing parents left England to move to the United States. Upon arrival, before being permitted to leave the Queen Elizabeth I, immigration officials checked the health of all immigrants.

"When they found out I was deaf," writes Dr. Leigh, *"they refused to allow me entry on the*

grounds that my deafness would cause me to be a burden to the country."

The family was sent to Ellis Island, which at that time was a holding facility for those seeking entry into the U.S., to await a hearing the next day.

"During the hearing, my parents attempted to prove that I was capable and my deafness would not be a barrier. They wrote instructions on drawing paper to 'draw a house' or 'draw a tree' which I did.

"The judge in charge of the hearing watched my efforts, proclaimed his grandchild of the same age could not even do what I had done, and allowed my parents to take me into the U.S. Concluded Dr. Leigh, "Hence, as my parents like to say, I got them into Ellis Island and I got them out."

Hospitals often put the sign "Deaf Mute over a deaf patient's bed. *"One deaf woman I know,"* writes Alice Campbell Amann, *"was not too happy about it and asked her nurse to put a 'C' over the 'M' . . . then it read 'Deaf Cute'."*

Hearing Aids

The most ancient "hearing aid" was probably one's own hand cupped behind the ear.

The earliest ear trumpets were made of horns of cows. Later on trumpets became fancier and were sometimes embedded with gems.

The first known British patent for a hearing aid was made in 1836. In 1902 electric hearing aids were being manufactured and sold. These required two large batteries: one a large, heavy, wet cell storage

battery, the other a slightly smaller dry cell. Deaf women used to lug around heavy hearing aids camouflaged to look like purses; later they wore them inside their brassieres.

In the early 1950's, Zenith manufactured the pocket-sized single unit aid that sold for a mere $75.00. By late 1954 the first eye-glass hearing aids were put on the market; next came the behind-the-ear models. The latest all-in-the-ear aid style can barely be seen. Research is now focusing on cochlear implants which are surgically implanted behind the ear.

In the early years, false pride prevented many hard-of-hearing youngsters from using ear trumpets, but wealthy elders in those days had fancy jeweled ear trumpets.

Holly Elliot is an author/editor for the UC Center on Deafness in San Francisco. She became deaf

Illustrated by Ruth R. Peterson.

as a young adult and has been a recipient of a cochlear implant. Her progress is being monitored by computer at Duke University, Durham, N.C.

Sandra Ammons-Rasmus tells of still another use for a hearing aid:

"Back in the early 1970's, the dress code at my school in Maryland required dresses, but permitted miniskirts (pant-suits had yet to make an appearance).

The school audiologist fitted my whole class for an experiment with a new line of hearing aids. The earmolds were connected by wire to a mirror-like silver box that easily attached to the front of our blouses, dresses or shirts.

One day one of the girls in the class was astounded when one of the boys got the color of her 'panties-of-the-day' correct. Before I knew it, I was one of the victims. This continued for several days as the girls struggled to figure out how the boys could so accurately predict the colors? We found out when we caught a classmate taking his hearing aid out of his shirt pocket and lowering it under a girl's miniskirt in the back, using it as a reflector. We were flabbergasted! We were the victims of a 'panties-of-the-day' pool the boys set up."

Judith Pachciarz was the official physician at the 1985 World Games for the Deaf in Los Angeles.

Becoming deaf at the age of two-and-a-half with encephalomeningitis, it took her 41 years to overcome all the obstacles in her path to becoming a physician.

Frustrated by locked doors to higher education because of her deafness, she earned a Ph.D. in Microbiology — as close to Medicine as she could get. Then through more determination and more perseverance she was finally allowed to earn her Doctor of Medicine degree.

An electronics technician friend helped by modifying a portable oscilloscope that was to be her substitute for a stethoscope. It was a major breakthrough for Judith.

Judith Pachciarz is one of approximately ten deaf physicians in the United States and the first woman to obtain both an MD and a PhD. Reprint from Gallaudet Today.

Lydia Marie Seebach Abbott Waters, has been a programmer-analyst for 20 years in Baltimore. Her company has changed its name several times: Maryland Hospital Association, Hospital Shared Computer Corporation, Automatic Data Processing Inc., Pantamation Enterprises, Inc., Ferranti Data Systems, Ferranti Health Care Systems.

Lydia is in complete charge of the main-frame payroll systems for the many hospitals using that service.

Illustrated by Ruth R. Peterson.

Mothers

MOTHERS

Mothers—Our Dedicated Mothers

An effort was made to list the deaf mothers of successful children, both deaf and hearing. The roster grew geometrically. To these dear deaf mothers, our love and gratitude.

Mother:—
    She gave you life,
        helped choose your name,
    She watched you grow
        and took the blame
    when you did wrong.

Mother:—
    She dried your tears,
        she washed your clothes,
    She helped you cope
        with them and those,
    and went along.

Mother:—
    When it came time
        to cut the string,
    She let you go
        to do your thing,
        and hid her tears.

Mother:—
    Still, on her day
        we gather 'round
    To share the love
        that we have found
    can last for years.

Kathleen Schreiber
May 1988

Previous page. Photo credit: Glasby and Wood, 1945.

Mary Toles Peet

Mary Toles Peet (1836–1901), mother of **Elizabeth Peet**, wrote many poems for the delight of her acquaintances. Through the efforts of Elizabeth, Mary's alma mater, Fanwood—New York School for the Deaf, issued a volume of 188 pages of her verses in 1903. A year after her graduation with highest honors, she became the wife of Dr. Isaac Peet, Principal of the school in 1854.

For 26 years, **Anna Plapinger** (1891–1984) was the only deaf teacher in the country who taught during her time at an oral school, at the Lexington School for the Deaf (her alma mater). Now and then the women would return to "Mother Channa" and show their appreciation. Her life served as a lifelong role model for the women including her two daughters, **Dorothy Polakoff** and **Shirley Stein**.

Because Yvonne Pitrois' mother thought that her daughter was the only deaf person in the world, formal education took place at home. As early as 1914, Yvonne believed that deaf children of all nations must be taught history of the deaf and their friends. She wrote many articles for *The Silent Worker* starting in 1912.

Mary I. Doughtery Havens, Gallaudet 1908, was a protege of Sarah Harvey Porter who was a teacher at the Kendall School. Mary later became a teacher at the American School in Hartford. She is the mother of Catherine Havens Pumphrey, Gallaudet 1935; grandmother of Nancy Lee Davis Schmidt, Gallaudet E-1958; great-grandmother of Barbara Schmidt Supalla, Gallaudet 1980.

Nancy Lee Davis Schimdt reported that her grandmother, Mary Doughtery Havens, once visited a fortune teller who told her that she would meet a widower with three children. Two summers later she met and married a widower with four children and she raised all children like her own.

The deaf mother of E. R. Wright entered the Texas School in 1884. Her son, after serving in the state legislature, accepted appointment as Superintendent of the Texas School in the early 1940's.

Lon Chaney, the noted actor with a gift for facial expression, was known as *The Man of a Thousand Faces*.

When he was very young, his deaf mother was stricken with rheumatism and could not move her fingers. He read his mother's messages in her eyes and conveyed to her his own in facial and body language known as sign language.

Alice T. Brandt's "old fashioned" mother made arrangements through a mutual friend to match her with Irwin Brandt but they were already dating and were married a year later.

Ruth Katzen Goodstein formerly of Bronx, New York, has two children, Roslyn (Rosen) and Harvey, with Ph.D.s and a grandson (Jeff Rosen) who is a deaf lawyer. Jeff was one of the behind-the-scenes leaders during the Deaf President Now demonstrations at Gallaudet in 1988.

"Our children have their own feelings," said Ruth Ricker Peterson *"about having deaf parents. But I am sure they are satisfied."*

Dot Marsh Schwartzman was a housemother at the Western Pennsylvania School for over 30 years. She was "always there" for her girls, 24 hours a day. Her influence left a big impact on young ladies who were under her care. Dot is now retired but she does some volunteer work at convalescent hospitals.

Navy Lieutenant (j.g.) Allison P. Rhodes was killed in the Solomon Islands during World War II. In his memory, his deaf mother, Annie Crisp (Mrs. G. E.) Rhodes, of

Cedar Spring Museum, South Carolina. Annie Crisp Rhodes christening the Navy ship in Houston, TX. Courtesy of J. Charlie McKinney.

Walhalla, South Carolina, launched the USS Rhodes, a destroyer escort (DE) at the Brown Shipbuilding Company in Houston, Texas.

When Ida Vernon lost her husband in 1975, her six children encouraged her to go to Gallaudet College. Her local Vocational Rehabilitation office refused to pay for her tuition because she was 62 years old. The National Center for Law and the Deaf on Kendall Green, took up the cudgels as it was a discrimination case based on her age.

Ida was graduated in 1981 with a Bachelor of Arts degree in Social Work on her 67th birthday. She has been a "Dorm Mom" at MSSD and a Camp Mark VII volunteer at Father Thomas Coughlin's camp in Old Forge, N.Y. She currently is doing missionary work in Hawaii.

In Linda Hatrak Cundy's column "Mother Knows Best" in the *NAD Broadcaster,* she writes:

"I lay my curse (on) the pediatricians for misleading parents into thinking that their babies would soon learn to speak regardless of degree of hearing loss.

"Parents need to know right away that there is some chance that their hearing-impaired children might not learn to pronounce words intelligibly and that there are other alternatives to consider. Mother knows best; I rest my case."

Esther Dockter Frelich, mother of nine deaf children, has long been active in volunteer community work with both deaf and hearing in her hometown, Devils Lake, North Dakota. Phyllis, the actress, is the oldest child in the family.

"I would never want to trade our nine deaf children for hearing children," says Esther. *"They laughed, talked, played and got*

mad just like other children. We love them."

Another mother of nine children is **Della Caldonia Wilding** of Gooding, Idaho.

A deaf widow at the age of 81, **Mildred Lewis**, taught manual communication to Elizabeth Landfried's second-grade class at Redeemer Lutheran School, Austin, Texas, in the early 1980's. The children called her "Grandmother."

Louise Fletcher is the daughter of **Estelle Fletcher** of Alabama. In 1975 Louise won the Best Actress Award for her role in the motion picture *One Flew Over the Cuckoo's Nest.* She made her acceptance speech in voice and in sign language so that her folks could understand the message. *"I want to thank you,"* she signed and spoke, *"for teaching me to have a dream."*

Maurine Barron of Iowa, is the mother of two daughters, Stacia and LuAnn and two sons, all of whom participated in the XV World Games of the Deaf.

Catherine Bronson Higgins, a mother of triplet boys, accompanied her husband Francis Higgins on many Gallaudet tours abroad before she passed away. A son, Paul C. Higgins, wrote *An Outsider in a Hearing World.*

Camilla Sue Lange wrote a winning letter among 526 entries — *Why I Think Mother is the Best in the World.* The prize was a Mother's Day weekend for the entire family in the Andrew Johnson Hotel Penthouse in Knoxville, Tennessee in 1968.

Leaving NTD in the late 1960's after spending two years with the theatre troupe, actress June Russi Eastman found her role as the

mother of two daughters was to be cherished.

Margaret Hatch Baldridge, a teacher's aide at the Indiana School, is the proud mother of two fine daughters who are in the field of education of the deaf. **Sandra "Bunny" Klopping**, wife of California School (Fremont) Superintendent Dr. Henry Klopping, is the co-ordinator of the sign language program at Ohlone College. Kathryn "Kitty" Baldridge is a Physical Education instructor at Gallaudet.

Jane Miller shared her rich experiences as a foster mother in the February, 1974 issue of *The Deaf American.*

Helen Hammons, now of California, spent a lifetime raising a family in Pensacola, San Diego, Honolulu and Alameda while her career Navy husband, a Chief Machinist's Mate, was being transferred from station to station. She raised three girls and a boy and now enjoys seven grandchildren;

some close by in California, a few in Illinois and one great-grandchild in Illinois.

In the early 1970's, Helen Hammons was the first editor of the San Francisco-Oakland DAN (Dial-A-News). Robert Weitbrecht, deaf inventor of the TTY/TDD coupler, persuaded Helen to house the DAN equipment in her Alameda, CA home. The only space available was in her bedroom. The DAN being available 24 hours 7 days a week to TTY callers made sleep impossible for Helen's hearing husband. He could not get a good night's sleep due to in-coming calls at all hours of the night. After about a year's effort, Helen turned over her editorial duties to Edward Ingram of San Mateo, CA. Mr. Ingram served the DAN about eight months before leaving for Southern California to pursue higher education opportunities. Oakland (CA) resident

Judith Rasmus Bravin's family in New York State. Courtesy of Gallaudet Archives.

George Attletweed then took over the reins of the SFO DAN and served 14 years before equipment malfunctioning problems necessitated closing down the DAN system. George's wife, **Bernadette Gallagher Attletweed,** gave much support during his tenure as editor. She hopes that the DAN concept will be restored in the near future when new technology can be applied by enterprising deaf people — possibly a deaf woman!

Judith Rasmus Bravin, head librarian at New York School for the Deaf, accompanied and tutored her son, Jeff, while in Los Angeles. He was appearing in *And Your Name is Jonah*. Her husband, Philip, is Chairman of the Board of Trustees of Gallaudet University.

Sue Kovacs, mother of Jonny Kovacs, a child star in *Second Family Tree* and other TV programs is another example. She moved to Los Angeles to be close to him during the filming days.

New In-Laws

Fred took me to Brooklyn, New York, to meet his family and to be perfectly honest, I had absolutely no knowledge about Jews and Gentiles.

When I was introduced to his feisty little 5'3" 80-year-old grandmother who had outlived five husbands, she stood before me and looked me in the eye. I did likewise, wondering what she was leading up to. Suddenly she nodded and turned away with a gesture to several other family members who followed her to pursue her favorite pastime — pinochle. She was one of the best players in all of Brooklyn.

A few years after our wedding in September, 1944, my mother-in-law told me what that first impression was all about. Fred's mother protested she did not want her son to marry a Gentile and her mother responded with, *"If that girl was brave enough to come to a house where she knew she was not wanted and look me in the eye like that, she's good enough to marry your son!"*

Grandma Bertha died shortly after our marriage and our first daughter, Beverly, has been named for her.

I can only echo the truth of that old saying, *"When ignorance is bliss, 'tis folly to be wise."*

—Kathleen "Kit" Schreiber

Vivian Joyce Barker—1940's

Mother, My Rescuer

Our family moved north in a covered wagon from our grandparents' homestead to a small farm in Nebraska.

One day my father left my mother and us three kids on the farm while he went to town for supplies.

A tornado hit us without warning. Mother was badly injured but she managed to find strength to look for us. She found my sister and brother quickly but they had to hunt for me.

She finally found me tightly rolled in a blanket and freed me in time to catch my breath. There was a wen behind my ear and Mother claimed that it caused my deafness.

—Vivian Joyce Barker

A Deaf Mother

"Shhhh! I know she can hear us . . . I think she's been fooling us . . . she's not deaf at all!" I can remember whispering those words to my twin sister as we jumped on our beds upstairs or stole treats from the cookie jar. What we didn't know then, but soon learned, was that our parents were deaf, but certainly not dumb.

My mother knew instinctively how to be a "super mom." She had a warm and loving relationship with her own mother and was naturally a warm and loving mother to us. Her deafness was not apparent to me until I was about five years old.

Sometimes the other kids would ask, *"How come your parents talk funny?"* My answer was always, *"They don't!"* so the problem became theirs, not mine.

In my house, stories were read, songs were sung and nursery rhymes were told in my mother's warm and soothing voice. Some say prelingually, profoundly deaf people can't sing. To me, her voice was the balm I needed at the end of my busy day.

The richness of my childhood speaks for itself. I am the lucky member of two cultures and the child of two loving, warm people.

—Ann MacIntyre Levesque

A Mother's Stories Retold

Hazel Pike Stakley

In the early 1900's, schools for the deaf sent special trains to collect deaf children in the fall, and send them back home in the same way at the end of the school year. The conductors took responsibility for chaperoning the children.

One fall, two very young first-year deaf girls were put on the train by their parents. Each girl had a name tag attached to her sweater button for proper identification. During the long ride the girls became warm and took off their sweaters while they played.

At the end of the ride the girls hurriedly grabbed their sweaters — unfortunately the garments were switched. The school officials met the train and identified each girl by the name tag attached to her sweater.

All through the school year the girls learned to speak and write "their names" and the school officials corresponded with the parents about the girls' progress and health problems.

In June the parents were shocked to find out that their little girls had different names and different parents.

There was a prayer meeting prior to classes every morning at the North Carolina School where my mother attended. A certain male teacher tended to drag his prayers out *"forever."* He closed his eyes when he prayed but his blind eye remained partly open.

Hazel Pike Stakley (1896–1977)

My restless mother would not dare to talk or move as she believed his *"evil"* eye was watching her.

There was a time when Alexander Graham Bell tried to have a bill passed that would forbid deaf people from marrying each other. He believed this was a means to reduce chances of their giving birth to deaf babies. Many deaf women students quit school to get married in a hurry to beat the *"deadline."* Fortunately, the bill never passed.

My mother was repeatedly warned by older peers at her school not to swallow fruit seeds or it would cause appendicitis. Thus she would be barren the rest of her life.

In the old days in many schools for the deaf, the older girls would take the responsibility of formal *"sex education"* to their younger peers. Eleven was the magic age to learn about sex.

There were 13 children in my mother's family. She was the tenth.

Every spring, the minute my mother got off the special train from school, her siblings would start to badger her for funny/sad dormitory or classroom experiences that happened during the school year. Often times her younger sisters wished they were deaf so they could join in the fun.

The "new" Fowler Hall at Gallaudet College was not ready for the preparatory girls in the fall of 1917, so the girls had to stay at home until October of that year. When they finally arrived at Gallaudet they had to stay in House #1.

During that time there was a company of U.S. soldiers camped in the field behind President Hall's home, House #1. My mother and her friends had fun passing notes back and forth with the homesick soldiers.

To prove his love, a boy would eat a whole apple — seeds, core and all — for his girl friend at a state residential school.

Mine, Mine

Jennie Jones, a classmate at the North Carolina School and a roommate in Akron, Ohio, was an all-around athlete during World War I. She once went to a company picnic with a date who asked her to pretend to lose some games.

Jennie agreed but won all contests anyway. She sobbed in distress as she explained that she tried to lose but something in her would not allow her to do so. She offered to return some of the prizes but the judges would not take them.

During bygone days at many residential schools for the deaf, the girls could take a bath only once a week. In between baths they powdered themselves liberally with talcum powder.

Then the boys would fool the girls in some way to make them show possession of something in sign language. The girls would slap on their chests and say, *"Mine, mine!"* The boys enjoyed watching the powder billowing out of their necklines.

There were other boys who did the same thing but they were more interested in which bosoms were real and which were stuffed with powder puffs.

Mary L. Thornberry Hearing and Speech Center at Gallaudet was named in honor of deaf mother of former Congressman Homer Thornberry of Texas. He was also a Judge of the United States Court of Appeals, First District.

Oh, Deaf ... Impossible!

During the 1930's, my family would spend one week of the summer vacation at a resort in northern Wisconsin. It was customary to spend time getting acquainted with the other guests in the big hotel. We would sit together in the dining room and participate in planned activities.

During the week some of the guests began to talk and had doubts about my family. Through the grapevine, they heard that I

Evelyn Lipshutz Zola

was deaf. Others denied it saying, *"Oh, no, that's impossible. This young girl acts just like all the other children."* Then one lady stated, *"I am going to find out for myself."*

One day she made arrangements with my mother to take me on a hike. My mother was surprised that a woman we had just met would want to take me with her. I did not want to go but my mother persuaded me to join this lady.

"Why," I thought to myself, *"do I have to go with this old lady? I have nothing in common with her. Maybe she has no friends."*

I expected the lady to lead the way but she wanted me to go first. I was proud of what I had learned in Girl Scouts and followed the markings on the birch trees and the worn path through the woods.

I was concentrating on the trail ahead but every once in a while I would turn around to make sure that the old lady was still following me. Every time I looked back the lady would smile knowingly.

We spent the entire morning hiking on the wilderness trail that finally ended back at the resort. The old lady spotted my mother and ran up to her saying, *"Your daughter is not deaf; it is impossible!"*

My mother questioned, *"Why do you think that?"* The lady explained, *"While we were walking, I called out Evelyn's name. Every time I called it, she would turn around and look at me."*

—Evelyn Lipshutz Zola

It is indeed very difficult writing a tribute to my Mom, **Hedy Udkovich** and my Ronma, **Ruth O. Stern**, as they have shaped my life in more ways than can be described by mere words.

I certainly cannot visualize being the contented woman I am now without the loving guidance of my dearest Mother — who opened up many doors for me — that of the incredible deaf world, that of the fascinating world of books, that of growing up into glorious womanhood and also that fulfilling world of motherhood (with three beautiful deaf children). Ronma, besides giving me the gift of her son, added the final touches to my way of life, my way of thinking and my way of loving.

—Hedy Udkovich Stern

Pink Refrigerator

Georgia Black Canady, a product of North Carolina and a current resident of Los Angeles, produced nine beautiful deaf children. Shortly after the father had a heart attack, he was laid off his job.

Mary, the second daughter,

Esther Dockter Frelich's family in North Dakota. Courtesy of Priscilla Frelich.

wrote to Jack Bailey, the TV host of *"Queen For A Day"* about her father's mishap and the family's financial problems. Her deaf siblings needed school clothes and money for train fares from Los Angeles to Berkeley.

Mary was invited appear on the TV show to try for the title on December 24, 1956. She won and was crowned *"Queen For A Day."* The siblings received nice school clothes and toys-toys-toys. Mary received 12 pairs of shoes, lingerie and many other gifts; also a choice of a pink or white refrigerator. Georgia, had to live for the next

30 years with the pink one Mary selected.

It was one of the best Christmases ever for the family. More gifts kept on coming to the house for the next several months.

Ann Garretson Benedict was the general chairman of the 1965 AAAD Basketball Tournament in Cincinnati. She felt badly about neglecting her young deaf children, Holly Duve and Dwight Benedict, during those evenings so she hired a reliable babysitter every night. There was some kind of surprise, play activity for them.

One evening a home movie was shown where Ann explained to the children in sign language that she loved them dearly and she missed them.

Another evening it was a "Treasure Hunt" where her babysitter drove them all over the city and visited people they knew to collect their treasures.

Proud are the mothers of the leaders of the peaceful protest at Gallaudet University in March, 1988:

a) **Margaret O'Gorman Hlibok** of New York City, mother of Greg Hlibok, the newly elected Student Body President. He was a guest on Ted Koppel's *Nightline,* the ABC-TV show. A month later, his sister Nancy was crowned Miss Junior NAD at the 1988 convention in Fremont, California. Greg was later named the "Person of the Week" by ABC's Peter Jennings.

b) Nancy Bloom Rarus Shook of Virginia, mother of the outgoing Student Body President Tim Rarus. Tim was praised on several national interviews for his leadership in keeping students under control during the protest.

c) Patricia Hageage Covell of Washington, mother of Jerry Covell, a former student body officer. Jerry was in the lead at the rallies with his graphic signs. TV cameras caught him leading the chanting of *"Deaf President Now"* and *"There Are Many More Doors to Open Yet."*

d) Bridgetta Belle Bourne of Washington, daughter of Jenny Sue Burton Borne, was noted for her strong "voice" protesting the injustice of a non-deaf president at Gallaudet and her leadership in strategic planning. She signed (aloud) on national TV, *"We want to be free from hearing oppression. We don't want to live off the hearing world; we want to live as independent people."*

Children of Deaf Parents—Deaf President NOW leaders. Courtesy of Angel Ramos of Deaf America Show. Photo by Tom Samuals.

Organizations

ORGANIZATIONS

National Association of the Deaf

Displaying early symbols of tokenism, a slight nod to the distaff members of the deaf community, the NAD elected a few women to the office of second vice president: **Cloa Lamson** of Ohio in 1920; **Mrs. C. A. Jackson** of Atlanta in 1923; and **C. Belle Rogers** of Cedar Springs, S.C., in 1926.

In celebration of its Centennial Year (1980), Gertrude Scott Galloway was elected the first woman president of the NAD.

"Upon becoming the first woman to be the president of the NAD in 100 years," jokes Gertie, *"I announced that I would first get rid of all men from the NAD and then I would burn my bra.*

"Then after giving the deaf men some time to worry a bit," she chuckled, *"I would say, 'Of course, I can't do that since I need both for support'."*

Effie W. Anderson is a renowned figure in education as well as the deaf community. She taught at several schools for the deaf where her husband, Dr. Tom L. Anderson, served as Principal.

The Andersons finally ended their travels and put down roots at the California School in Berkeley. During her husband's two terms as

Previous Page. 1987's Deaf Women United Pre-Conference Training meetings for the facilitators—Front row, from left to right: L. Bonheyo, E. Aviles, E. Roth, S. Emery, G. Galloway. Second row, from left to right: S. Williams, J. Berke, I. Leigh, N. Lewis, F. Vold, M. Holcomb. Third row, from left to right: L. Crook, H. Williamson, C. McCaskill-Emerson, D. Copeland, C. Massey and J. Slone. (Not pictured: Rachel Stone-Harris.) Courtesy of Deaf Women United.

Girl Scouts of the Alabama School for the Deaf at Talladega–1924. Courtesy of Gallaudet Archives.

President of the NAD, 1940–46, Effie reigned as the First lady.

Caroline Hyman Burnes took over as First Lady in 1947 when Byron B. Burnes was elected President.

The role shifted when the NAD elected its first Executive Secretary, and **Kathleen Bedard (Mrs. Fred) Schreiber** reigned as First Lady from 1966 to 1979.

Junior N.A.D.

Caroline Hyman Burnes, the librarian of the California School in the 1960s, envisioned the establishment of a Junior NAD. In a short time, officers of the NAD brought the idea to fruition with

the formal recognition of the Jr. NAD program.

Melinda Chapel Padden hailed from Indiana. She was the first chairperson of the Midwestern Youth Leadership Demonstration at the Indiana School where she was the original member of Jr. NAD. A freshman at Gallaudet, she was chosen to represent the deaf youth at large on the Youth committee of the President's Committee on the Employment of the

Girl Scouts of the Missouri School for the Deaf at Fulton–1950. Courtesy of Gallaudet Archives.

Handicapped in the year 1971. A great lover of the outdoors, she was appointed the Youth Leadership Camp Director.

Virginia Pusser Culpepper (South Carolina School) and Virginia Bethke (Wisconsin School) were the first members of the Deaf Student Exchange Program sponsored by the Jr. NAD in 1969. The program was not continued after a one-year experiment.

Oddly, these two girls never met until 1980 at the Jr. NAD Convention at Gallaudet.

Joanne Hamblin Williams, now living in Hawaii, was the first female camp director of Youth Leadership Camp in Pengilly, Minnesota, in 1979. She was the Jr. NAD co-ordinator from 1978 through 1983, and the advisor of the Jr. NAD Conference. Joanne became deaf through birth injury; attended oral programs through her adolescent years; learned sign language at the age of 23.

National Fraternal Society of the Deaf "The Frat"

The National Fraternal Society of the Deaf (NFSD) was founded in 1901 by a group of male students at the Michigan School. It was originally called *"Coming Men of America."* Women were not welcome as it was argued that a woman's place was at home.

A group of deaf feminists during the early 1920s voted to start NAD-FRAT Women's Club in Atlanta, Georgia because they were not accepted equally by deaf men of either the NAD or FRAT.

Gertrude Sattery Elkins, first woman to be insured by "The Frat." Reprint from News-Herald, Morganton, North Carolina.

A drive for a clubhouse to be the first ever built by an organization of deaf women started in 1925. Mrs. C. L. Jackson was the leader of the fund-raising project and an appeal was printed in *The Silent Worker* in 1925.

Social auxiliaries (Aux Frats) were founded in 1937 and continued until the 1950's when women were accepted as regular members of The Frat.

In 1921, Mrs. Annie Lashbrook, printing instructor at the Rome, New York School, was the President of the Empire State Association of the Deaf. One of her promises on her election was to confront the NFSD to force them to admit women.

The Frat was closed to deaf women for 53 years until Gertrude Slattery Elkins, of Kentucky, was admitted in 1954.

Mary Longlois Woods Berstein of Baton Rouge, Louisiana, was the first deaf woman to hold a full-time position with the NFSD. She was elected to the office of Grand (National) Secretary.

Registry of Interpreters for the Deaf

Celia Burg Warshawsky (1921-1986) was the first deaf holder of a

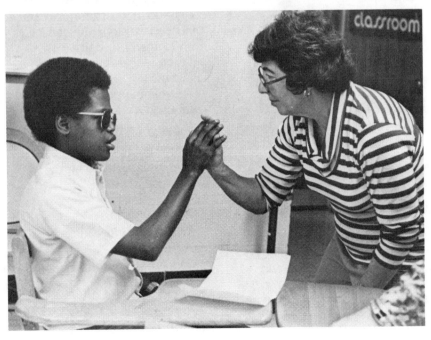

Celia Warshawsky interpreting for deaf-blind client. Gallaudet Photo Lab.

Reverse Skills Certificate (RSC) to be active in RID. She served as Vice President for two terms.

Celia Warshawsky, Edna Adler, Evelyn Zola, Marjoriebell Holcomb, Ruth Sandefur Yates, Anna Marie Rinaldi, Barbara Babbini Brasel and Mikki Simpson were deaf women who served on the RID Board between 1964 and 1986.

Quota International

Quota International, a professional women's service club, initiated the *Shatter Silence* program and the annual *International Deaf Woman of the Year* award.

Ruth Gustafson Ludovico, of Pittsburgh, was the first deaf member of Quota International. She persuaded friends in the Washington, D.C. area, Agnes Minor Padden, Barbara Myer Stevens, and Julia Burg Mayes to join this organization.

The winners of the Quota International Woman-of-the-Year award are:

1978 Irene Tunanidas
1979 Angela Petrone Stratity
1982 Alberta Delozier Smith
1983 Celia Burg Warshawsky
1987 Solange Sevigny Skyer

Deaf Women United

The first National Deaf Women's Conference was held at Santa Monica, California, the summer of 1985. The theme was Deaf Women United which was adopted as the official name of the organization the following year.

Seven women from different parts of the country were elected to the steering committee and instructed to develop by-laws and be incorporated by September, 1987.

DWU Conference Goals

The goals developed by the Conference committee were as follows:

1) learn more about ourselves as deaf women; communicate our needs; develop inner resources to meet those needs
2) acknowledge and accept the diversity of individual deaf women; explore how the experience of being deaf, and being women, affects our lives
3) empower women to commit to positive changes by determining how to take control of their lives
4) formally establish Deaf Women United and share vision and resources needed to empower other women in our local communities

---

The second DWU Conference, held at George Mason University, Fairfax, Virginia in August, 1987, was sponsored by DeafPride, an organization incorporated in 1972.

Katherine Jankowski was the conference coordinator; Barbara Kannapell assisted by Eileen Paul from Women's Technical Assistance, conducted group process activities.

The members of the original committee were:

Allie Joiner, Chairwoman, Seattle
Christine Buchholz, Los Angeles
Sheila Conlon Mentkowski, Greenbelt, Md.
Betty G. Miller, Washington, D.C.
Marcia Kessler Nowak, Westbury, N.Y.
Sandra Ammons-Rasmus, Fremont, Calif.
Gwendolyn Speaks, Little Rock, Ark.

Metropolitan Washington Association of the Deaf

The Metropolitan Washington Assn. of the Deaf (MWAD) celebrated its 50th Anniversary in the Fall of 1987.

The historian reported that the first club was the Capitol Silent Club (1920–23); then the Washington Silent Club (1925–1928); then the District of Columbia Silent Athletic Club (1935–1944); the District of Columbia Club of the Deaf (1945–1966); and finally the Metro name currently in use.

The first deaf woman member was Daisy D'Onfrio, and the first women to hold office were Minnie Bache and Dorothy Havens.

Mary Canady Noble of California, the first deaf woman president of the DCARA Board, helped the agency expand from a staff of only two to 55 during her tenure. She is now a real estate investor.

Elizabeth (Bets) Douglas Ailstock was the first president of the Ladies' Auxiliary of the Brooklyn Association of the Deaf.

The American Association of Retired Persons (AARP) awards scholarships each year to Elderhostels. This is a program at colleges all over the country in which older Americans study various subjects for one week.

Charlotte Halperin Collums won a 1987 scholarship and spent a week at Gallaudet in June. Her selection for the award was based on her activities with the deaf senior citizens in Little Rock, Arkansas. According to the news release, the competition for the scholarship was intense.

A native of Iowa, **Shirley McLeland Hicks**, was the first woman president (1985) of the Iowa Association of the Deaf in 100 years. She was also the recipient of the *Best Teacher-of-the-Year* award from the University of Iowa in 1987.

Sharon Crawford Hovinga, from Texas, is another leader in that area. She arranged the first conference for Midwestern Deaf Women in Omaha, Nebraska in May, 1987. She has held several important offices in the NAD.

Cheryl Lynn Weisgerber Alessi, originally from New Jersey, president of the South Carolina Association, and **Helen Brant Maddox**, native of South Carolina, were instrumental leaders in the Palmetto State. They made it possible to set up the Home Office with a full-time Executive Director in 1983 on the campus of South Carolina School for the Deaf and Blind with the appropriation for the Home Office being given as a line item in the SCSDB budget. The organization purchased and moved into its own home office building in Columbia, S.C. in 1986.

Cheryl was appointed the 1988 NAD Convention Fiscal Manager. Helen was the founder of the *South Carolina NEWS* (monthly newsletter) in the 1960's.

The machinery for the establishment in California of the first Home Office was accomplished during **Lillian Hahn Skinner's** (1975–1977) presidency.

Joyce MacNab is one of the nation's known deaf trainers of EARS FOR THE DEAF, a hearing ear dog training agency in Michi-

Cheryl L. Alessi. Photo by J. Keel.

gan. She oversees a group of dogs and trainers.

The National Conference for Deaf and Hearing Impaired Postal Workers, under the auspices of the American Postal Workers Union, took place in April, 1988 at Washington, D.C. **Karen Atwood** of Seattle and **Debi McNally** of Michigan coordinated workshops featuring filing a grievance, working with interpreters, agreement rights, safety and health, parliamentary procedures, steward training and assertiveness training for the first time in history.

Honors

Deirdre Kennedy Ritter, a high school language arts teacher at California School for the Deaf, Fremont, was named *1986 California Teacher of the Deaf* by the National Center on Deafness at California State University, Northridge.

Madeline Mussmano (1976); **Carol Billone** (1982); and **Bernadette Gallagher Attletweed** (1983) were previously honored.

Anne Garretson Benedict won many prizes and awards for her fashion designs which she modeled herself. She received training at Stephens College, Columbia, Missouri.

Although she was the only deaf student, she managed to participate in college activities. She made excellent progress in fashion designing classes at this exclusive women's college and was graduated in the 1940's.

Donna Pocobello was the 1983 recipient of the Rochester Institute of Technology Eisenhart Award for outstanding teaching. She has been a sign communication specialist at National Technical Institute for the Deaf in Rochester. There are over 850 faculty members at RIT-NTID.

"Teaching goes beyond fulfilling the charges placed upon me in my profession," stated Donna Pocobello. *"Teaching is a way of life. There are 'born teachers.' Teaching is leading the student to the realization of many purposes in life."*

Iva Boggs Eklof was recognized by the Wisconsin legislature in 1985 for her excellence as the first deaf teacher to be hired to teach in a public day school in the state. She retired after 17 years of teaching.

Rachel Naiman, from New York, was named Outstanding Professor for 1986-87 at Front Range Community College in Colorado. She has been an interpreter training instructor since 1981.

The Laurent Clerc Cultural Fund under the auspices of the Gallaudet University Alumni Association provides four annual awards given for meritorious achievement: One is the Alice Cogswell

Award for valuable service in behalf of deaf people.

The **Dorothy Morrison Jacobs Memorial Community Award** is given every year in the San Francisco Bay Area. The honor goes to the person who has contributed and kept a low profile in his/her community work without compensation except for necessary expenses.

Kathleen Dowling of Fremont, California, was the first recipient of this DMJ Award in 1978.

Betty-Jo Raines Lependorf was honored several times for her volunteer work with the deaf-blind in the San Francisco Bay Area. In 1980 she was the third recipient of the Dorothy Morrison Jacobs Memorial Community Award.

The recipients were:

1978 Kathleen Dowling
1979 Alvah Reneau
1980 Betty-Jo Raines Lependorf
1981 Georgia Telecky
1982 Bernice Hoare (and Julian) Singleton
1983 June Lampe
1984 Charlotte Whitacre
1985 Aurelia Ratto
1986 Betty June King Bentz
1987 Helen West Chism

Tennessee's **Jane Ann Shelton** was given an honorary graduation diploma at Tennessee School for the Deaf in 1988 for her numerous accomplishments in her home state. Former president of the Tennessee Association of the Deaf, she served on the Executive Board of the NAD during the term of 1986–1988. As a lobbyist, she obtained increased funding from the state legislature for the five communication centers under the auspices of the Council for the Deaf in the state.

Sororities

Phi Kappa Zeta

In the 1880's, debates were an important part of college education. The women students were allowed to observe the men students discussing important issues. Not being allowed to join them, the women students started a literary society (1892) late at night on the first floor of the president's home, where they read poetry, discussed literature and held debates in a secretive manner. Eventually the secret debating group became Phi Kappa Zeta sorority. **Agatha Tiegel**, one of the 13 founding members, became the first president of the first national sorority.

Adele Jensen Krug, from Minnesota, was an associate Professor of Library Science at Gallaudet in the 1950s and 1960s. During her term as the national President of the O.W.L.S., she suggested that the organization change its name to a Greek one.

The historic Gallaudet sorority adopted the Hellenic name of Phi Kappa Zeta and the first Rush season at Gallaudet was held during the 1954–55 year. At that time the colors were changed from brown and gold to blue and white.

Delta Epsilon

Delta Epsilon Sorority was founded on Kendall Green in 1953 with the purpose of encouraging good scholarship, high moral integrity, friendship and leadership, and to pursue philanthropic projects.

Phi Delta Espilon (Chi Omega Psi)

Chi Omega Psi Sorority was organized in 1970. The purpose is to serve the deaf, the community, and Gallaudet University; to encourage academic excellence; and to promote civic responsibility, social maturity and leadership.

The Silver Star Club

The Silver Star Club, a sorority for young ladies at the Ohio School was organized in the early 1900s.

The girls were encouraged to have the proper spirit in life and an understanding of the meaning of charity was stressed. At one time the club clothed and fed three deaf French children in La Malgrange School near Nancy, in France, and five deaf Japanese orphans shortly after World War I.

Originally the S.S. Club was a secretive name and the boys were guessing it to be Silk Stockings, or Sun Shine, or Soft Shoulders.

One year a lover insisted that a member tell him the name to prove her love for him. Eventually the couple broke up and the real name, Silver Star, was revealed.

Opposite, Top: Delta Epsilon Sorority–1988 Homecoming Parade, "Bisonhood." Gallaudet Photo Lab.

Opposite, Bottom: Alumnae/Collegiate Sisters at PKZ banquet–1988. Gallaudet Photo Lab.

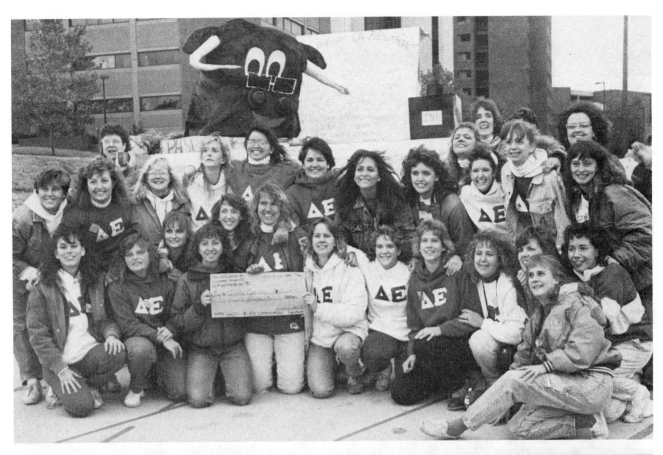

The first National Convention of Deaf Mutes in Ohio—1880. Courtesy of National Association of the Deaf, D.C. Redington.

The Silver Star Club of the Ohio School inviting the male students to the Roller Skating party—1940.

DEAF WOMEN

O.W.L.S. at Gallaudet College, circa 1938.
First row: H. Zola, Miss E. Benson, Miss E.
Nelson, E. Koob, Miss E. Peet, R. Clark,

L. Hahn. Second row: M. Forehand, O. Benoit,
F. May, N. Brannan, H. Henson, V. Byars. Third
row: B. Schiller, C. Marshall, M. Mazur,

L. Gamst, M. Albert, N. Corneliussen,
B. Marshall, I. Silverman. Courtesy of
Gallaudet Archives.

Melinda Chapel Padden coordinated the first
National Junior NAD Convention in Washington, DC–1970. Photo by the Foto Club.

Queens

QUEENS

Miss Deaf America

Susan Davidoff, 1976 winner, said *"At the end of my two years traveling as Miss Deaf America, and meeting such fine and dedicated people, my feet will be sore, my hands will be tired, my body will ache from fatigue—but, I will have learned a great deal."*

1972 **Ann Billington**, Gallaudet
1974 **Mary Pearce**, Mississippi
1974 **Pam Young**, Gallaudet
1976 **Susan Davidoff**, Maryland
1978 **Jacquelin Roth**, Maryland
1978 **Debra Krausa**, Pennsylvania
1980 **Mary Beth Barber**, New York
1982 **Barbara Tubbs**, New York
1984 **Margo Cienik**, California
1986 **Patricia Brennan**, Maine
1988 **Brandies Ann Sculthorpe**

The 1974 title holder, **Mary Pearce**, of Mississippi, relinquished her crown to the first runner-up, **Pam Young**, of Gallaudet. **Jacqueline Roth**, of Maryland, surrendered her tiara to **Debra Krausa**, of Pennsylvania, in 1978. Both Queens were married during their reigns.

Barbara Tubbs, 1982 Miss Deaf America, was a member of the Gallaudet Dancers. Her talent at the pageant was Baton Twirling.

Julie Rems, a student at the Cal-State, Northridge (CSUN), Miss California in 1985–87, is a chess whiz.

At the 1988 NAD Convention in Charleston, South Carolina, the bartender came up with a nonalcoholic drink special *"Strawberry Patty Cake"* in honor of past Miss

Previous Page. 1958 Homecoming Queen. Left to right: Melvia Miller, Texas; Carolyn Foley, Illinois; Joyce Jacobson, Iowa; Nancy Malone, New York.

Ann Billington Bahl '72

Deaf America, **Patricia Brennan**.

In the two years of her reign (1986–1988) she traveled extensively throughout the United States, serving as a role model for young people and promoting the skills and capabilities of deaf youths. Patty's advice to hearing parents of deaf children: *"Please keep an open mind as you explore the best education system for your deaf child. Remember that just because you put your deaf child into a hearing school, it does not mean that they will become hearing. It is also important to communicate with your child—don't set her/him aside from the activities of family life. Let your child learn and grow in a positive environment. And let her/him know that s/he can do anything s/he sets her/his mind to."* Reprinted from *"The Deaf Courier,"* 1988 NAD Convention Newsletter, Issue #4.

When Patty passed on the crown to Brandeis Ann Sculthrope during the Miss Deaf America Pageant, the outgoing queen's parents were coincidentally sitting next to the parents of the incoming queen.

Brandeis, a social worker major at NTID, said, *"I could not believe it when they called out my name as the winner, but it's great to be able to serve as a role model for the deaf community, especially for deaf children."* In the talent competition, she did a dramatic reading, *"A Message to America — Drinking and Driving Don't Mix."* Reprinted from *The News and Courier* (Charleston, South Carolina), July 9, 1988.

Miss Deaf America Pageant

By Frances Manzella Marloff

In 1982, Miss Deaf Ohio, **Sandra Frye**, while practicing her talent routine on stage late one evening, tripped and broke her ankle. In spite of this, she continued in the competition on crutches and was later voted Miss Congeniality.

In 1986, during rehearsals, a contestant tripped backward and tore a curtain — twice. The theatre billed the NAD for a new curtain worth $1,300.

A contestant broke a spaghetti strap on her evening gown a few seconds before the gown competition. Using MacGyver-type ingenuity, she scotch-taped it to her back and brought home the bacon with the Best Evening Gown trophy.

Julia Peterson with Bison Mascot.

Jane Norman was the first Mistress of Ceremonies at the 1976 NAD Pageant in Houston. **Sally Pat Dow** (1974), **Phyllis Fletcher** (1976), **Ruth Sandefur** (1978), and **Helen Johnson Peterson** (1988) were directors.

June Russi Eastman and Gilbert Eastman, of Maryland, were the first wife-husband team to emcee the Miss NAD Pageant — in Balti-

more in 1984. They were also the first wife-husband team to join the National Theatre of the Deaf — 1967. Both are products of the American School in Hartford.

At the 1974 AAAD Basketball Tournament in Los Angeles, **Mary C. Noble** by then the mother of five beautiful children — was voted Miss AAAD.

Helen Whisman—Senior Queen, 1987.

Helen Whisman of Indianapolis, won two Queen titles: (1) Senior Queen at the AAAD Tourney in Louisville, in 1984 and (2) Senior Citizen Queen of Marion County and a finalist in Indiana State competition the summer of 1986.

Kathy Wilson played guard on the Washington State School football team and was crowned

Miss 1985 Kentucky Stephanie Hamilton joins the Sunday Parade.

Homecoming Queen on the same day in 1985.

Geraldine Gibbons of Chicago, was elected Miss NFSD (The Frat) in 1926.

Julie Petersen of Seattle, was crowned Homecoming Queen during Gallaudet University Week in 1986.

Nilza Cedeno of Buffalo, New York, was crowned *Miss Hispanic* in 1978. Her talent presentation was a mime routine set to music. She used an interpreter during interviews. She said that winning was not the most important part of her participation in the pageant — it was making so many new friends.

Doris Wilding—Miss District of Columbia, 1980. Gallaudet Photo Lab.

Religion

RELIGION

Some of the first mentions of deafness appear in the Bible. Some references to these may be found in the parts of the Bible as given below:

Exodus 4:10–12
Leviticus 19:14
Isaiah 29:18, 19; 35:4-6; 43:5–9
Psalms 38:12–15; 58:3–5
Micah 7:14–17

The Public Broadcasting Service (PBS) Deaf Heritage series on TV in the 1970's showed that generally, before the growth of Christianity, handicapped people were treated cruelly. The Greeks and Romans even killed babies with obvious deformities.

The Hebrews protected the deaf but their laws grouped them with fools and children.

A typical story tells of an event that occurred in 685 A.D. when St. John of Beverly succeeded in teaching a deaf-mute to speak simply by making the sign of the cross on his tongue. Records do not again mention a deaf person for more than 800 years.

Not much information on religious work among deaf women had been mentioned until recently; thus this chapter seems weak because of the paucity of information. We must accept the fact that the deaf were generally ignored until Christianity developed.

The story of **Cornelia A. Lothrop** (1835–1852) did for the church missions among the deaf what the story of **Alice Cogswell** did for the

Sister Julia Tenerowicz of Cincinnati, one of the original members of this congregation of deaf women nuns. She resides at Mt. St. Joseph on the Ohio River. She worked as teacher and staff member at St. Rita's School for the deaf for over 50 years. Courtesy of Father Tom Coughlin.

Rose Rosman with her daughter, Esther.

cause of the education of the deaf; it aroused sentiment in favor of all benevolent efforts.

During her illness and confinement, Rev. Thomas Gallaudet (son of Thomas Hopkins and Sophia Fowler Gallaudet) came to her bedside often. It was then that the Rev. Gallaudet decided to start his missionary work which led to the establishment of St. Ann's Church in New York City.

The Knights and Ladies de l'Epee met in its Sixth National Convention in Pittsburgh, Pa., in 1924. The first convention was held in Chicago in 1912 with a dozen Catholic men in attendance. The meetings had grown by hundreds with the consolidation of Ladies de l'Epee. This society had the aim to get in touch with other Catholic deaf across the country. It also inspired the priests and bishops to take up the work among the deaf.
— *Catholic Deaf-Mute*

Bridget Hughes is generally considered the first deaf nun in America. Through the years, St. Rita School for the Deaf in Cincinnati has had deaf nuns teaching there. The Sisters of St. Francis of Assisi, St. Francis, Wisconsin admitted several deaf sisters in the early 1930's.

"In Der Nacht," a vision of deaf survivors of Nazi oppression produced by **Marla Petal** and **Michelle Barron**, was on exhibit at Gallaudet University, in the rotunda of the U.S. Senate on Capitol Hill and at the National Congress of Jewish Deaf 17th Biennial convention in Anaheim and other sites. The photographs covered the joys and struggles of **Rose Steinberg Feld** and her husband Max before and during the Holocaust. The story began from the school days at the Israelite School in Berlin to the

pain of separation. Rose now lives in California and is an active member of Temple Beth Solomon of the Deaf. It was the temple that approached Marla as the community organizer to do the narrative exhibit.

Dulane Woodhouse, in the 1970's, was the first deaf woman missionary of the Church of Jesus Christ of Latter-Day Saints (Mormon).

Lynn Gottlich, in the 1980's, was the first deaf woman to be a rabbinical candidate doing two years of internship with Jewish deaf people.

Virginia W. Nagel, of Philadelphia, was ordained in the Episcopal Church as Deacon in 1987 and hopes to be Priest in 1988.

Francine Aona Kenyon, a native of Hawaii, was ordained in the Methodist Church in May, 1986.

Ferne Savanick and her husband, deaf lip-readers, served deaf members as lay readers in the Pennsylvania Mennonite Church during the 1950's.

The year 1987 saw Sandra K. Lund from Indiana achieve a new milestone. She left her teaching position at the California School in Fremont to do missionary work for her church, Christian Deaf Fellowship in Los Angeles. In 1988 she went to Jamaica to teach hundreds of impoverished deaf children.

Lois Weiner heads the Judaica Captioned Film Center in Baltimore, Maryland.

They captioned the movie by the National Council of Jewish Women—Cleveland section's *"A Time to Remember."* The movie commemorates Shoah, the Hebrew term for Holocaust, through a commission from the producers.

Myrtle Morris, a native of Georgia, started her missionary work with deaf people in Cuba in 1984. She was sponsored by the Southern Baptist convention.

Bess Hyman, of Van Nuys, California, lost her hearing at a late age. She has given many hours of service to the deaf community and won the AARP Elderhostel Award for 1987 on the basis of her voluntary contributions.

Additionally, Bess was the editor of the *National Congress of Jewish Deaf* quarterly newsletter for eight years; served as the treasurer of Temple Beth Solomon of the Deaf for over 12 years; was assistant to the chief financial officer, 1985 World Games of the Deaf for three years; received the 1986 GLAD Distinguished Service Award; and earned a degree from Hunter College, N.Y.C.

Rebecca Rosenstein in 1919 was the first Jewish woman to be graduated from Gallaudet College.

Anna Plapinger personally financed the first National Congress of Jewish Deaf (N.C.J.D.) convention in 1956.

Edith Chaplan, one of four founders of the Hebrew Association of the Deaf (H.A.D.) of New York, served as secretary for four years. She was honored frequently with awards for her many years of hard work chairing fund-raising events.

Edith was involved with the purchase of the Holocaust Torah from England for religious groups as well as being in charge of Passover and High Holy Days services in New York since 1979. She studied for and was awarded a high school degree at the age of 57.

Edith was an original member of the H.A.D. Friday afternoons, she led the Jewish students to a Temple near the Lexington School

1965 in traditional habit and 1987 in modern habit. Sister Maureen Langton of New York City, CSJ, pastoral coordinator in deaf ministry for the Archdiocese of New York City and assistant executive director at Camp Mark Seven at the Mohawk in Old Forge, New York, since its beginning in 1978. She was awarded "Outstanding Pastoral Worker of the year" in 1988 by the International Catholic Deaf Association. She attended St. Joseph Institute for the Deaf in St. Louis, Missouri and graduated from the Academy of Our Lady in Peoria, Illinois.

for the Deaf. She wanted to see her community to appreciate the qualities of Judaism just as she got quality Jewish education from her parents. Excerpt from the *National Congress of Jewish Deaf Quarterly* by Bess Hyman, June 1984.

Marge Klugman is well known for her involvement with Temple Beth Solomon of the Deaf. She is better known for her leadership in continuing education (see Education).

Signs in Judaism by **Adele Kronick Shuart** was one of the NCJD projects in publicizing the proper Jewish signs which is beneficial to the Jewish community. This first of its kind offers materials and instructions on Judaism to rabbis, teachers, interpreters and parents.

The N.C.J.D. Hall of Fame, a list of individuals excelling in cate-gories of religious, civic, professional and athletic leadership, has awarded recognition to three deaf women. They are: **Anna Plapinger, Celia Burg Warshawsky** and **Betsy Blumenthal.**

Temple Beth Or of the Deaf in New York City celebrated its silver anniversary in 1987. It is believed that this group of women may be the most active hustlers in the nation. They annually honor the Woman-of-the-Year for her contribution to the community. The past honorees were:

1963 Celia Siegel
1964 Esther Benensen and
     Joan Berke
1965 Alice Soll
1966 Alice Brand
1967 Catherine Ebin
1968 Betty Oshman
1969 Dorothy Pakula

1970 Malvina Goldberg
1971 Edith Chaplan
1972 Anna Guttman
1973 Shirley Lerner
1974 Ruth Stern
1975 Marcia Cohen
1976 Sylvia Weinstock
1977 Beverly Finkelstein
1978 Irene Argule
1979 Randy Sue Levenson
1980 Roslyn Grant
1981 Minnie Horenstein
1982 Stella Granath
1983 Wendy Bachman and
     Adelle Meyers
1984 Joanne Gleicher Garas
1985 Barbara Gold
1986 Sheila Wadler

Dressing dolls for needy children, Young Women's Christian Association (YWCA), taken on the lawn in front of the old wing of Fowler Hall (demolished in 1916), circa 1914. Courtesy of Gallaudet Archives.

The Pious Union of Our Lady of Good Counsel.
All U.S.A. deaf women. The order is now
defunct. Four or five out of the original group
switched from this congregation of deaf nuns
to a congregation for hearing nuns called "Sisters of Charity of Ohio." Courtesy of Father
Tom Coughlin.

Little Sisters of Seven Dolores of Our Lady (Les
Soeurs des Sept-Douleurs de Notre Dame) in
Cartiersville, Quebec. A French-speaking congregation of deaf nuns in Montreal, founded in
April, 1887. Several U.S.A. deaf women
entered this congregation because many con-
vents in U.S.A. were not open to them. All of
the nuns had to learn French. Most of them
worked as domestics under the supervision of
the hearing Sisters of the Providence of
Quebec.

The typical religious habit of the deaf nun is
a habit commonly worn by novices of the Sisters of the Providence of Quebec during the
novitiate. After the novitiate, the hearing nuns
wear a different type of habit, while the deaf
women were given novice habits for the rest
of their lives as religious. Habits were modified
as shown in this picture. The number peaked
at 85 during the early 1950's. Today there are
only 34 left, and there has been no vocation or
new candidate for the last 30 years. Courtesy
of Father Tom Coughlin.

Sports

SPORTS

Women athletes wore long dresses in the early years. Eventually styles changed and they wore bloomers. Nowadays they wear only comfortable sports clothes to fit the activities.

The *Bloomer Costume* for women consisted of a close-sleeved jacket, a skirt extending slightly below the knee, and a pair of loose trousers gathered by elastic bands a little above the ankle, like harem pants.

About 1849, **Amelia Jenks Bloomer**, a leader of the *Women's Rights Movement* in the United States, advocated such a costume. She claimed it would emancipate women from the conventional attire of the day and add greatly to their health and comfort.

Few followed her example as the costume was unpopular and exposed its wearer to ridicule. Nevertheless, Bloomer's designs provided the opening for public acceptance of more functional dress, particularly in sports. Latter-day *bloomers* were modified and became popular. These resembled men's knickerbockers, and were standard gym clothes in American schools until after World War II.

Our grandmothers could imagine nothing more risque than bloomers. Fortunately they passed away before the itsy-bitsy yellow polka dot bikini became standard beach wear.

The first women's athletic team at Gallaudet College was organized in 1896. The basketball squad won three games while losing none. (Men's basketball at Gal-

laudet was added in 1904.)

Kate Feeley, red-haired Irisher from Utah, excelled on the gymnasium floor, the tennis court, and the swimming pool. At Gallaudet, she starred in all fields of sports in the early 1920s.

Another deafened athlete inducted into the *Helms Foundation Hall of Fame* (Los Angeles) was **Gertrude Ederle**. She was the first woman to swim the English Channel, breaking all men's records, in 1926.

There is a treacherous strait between Europe and Asia known as the Strait of Dardanelles—or Hellespont. In 1929, **Eleanor Studley**, of the United States, broke all records swimming across this strait in 80 minutes.

Lorraine "Polly" Veronica Brady captured two awards at the 2nd Annual Spirit and Sportsmanship Workshop at the University of Southern Mississippi in 1967. Polly was the first student from Gal-

Top: 1913–1914

Above: Given Long

Previous Page. Celine Lawler won a silver medal in the 200m fly at the XV World Games for the Deaf in Los Angeles–1985. Photo by Richard J. Schoenberg.

laudet and the only deaf participant among some 325 college students from 80 colleges and universities from 25 states. She did the pom pom routine and a Spirit Stick in the final competition. She was the captain of the cheerleaders at the Arizona School for the Deaf in Tucson.

Patty Lopez of California was the first deaf woman to win the Far West Golf Association of the Deaf Tourney in 1982, beating all men and women. Patty joined the professional golfers in 1983 and was one of the top 10 players selected to go to Japan for two weeks in 1985. Her best round in a tourney was 70 with 7 birdies.

Gwen Long of Memphis, Tenn., scored an average of 28 points per game in high school basketball. She was the first player ever to score 2000 points and to make AAA Girls Tennessee All-State Basketball team in 1986. She is only 5' 3" tall.

Holly Holman is the only deaf woman with a record fresh-water catch — an 18" long, 31-lb 8-oz. large-mouth bass caught in Arkansas in 1986.

Betsy Bachtel, who was honored as co-winner of the 1986 Athletic-of-the-Year award by the AAAD, won All-American honors in the NCAA Division III National Cross-Country Championships. She excelled in several races while representing Gallaudet. **Connie Johnson**, of Utah, was the co-recipient.

In the *Dee Cee Eyes* in 1987, four deaf women anglers, **Virginia Skinner, Barbara Capes,** and **Peggy Teal,** all of North Carolina; and **Patricia Rosiecki,** New Jersey, were lauded for their prize catches in the salt-water fishing derby.

The XIV World Games for the Deaf — Women's Volleyball Team.

As athletic director at the Metro Washington Association of the Deaf, **Shirley Christian** organized many programs during the 1980s. She serves also as a sportswriter for the local deaf publication *Dee Cee Eyes*. When elected secretary of the Southeast Athletic Association of the Deaf, in 1986, she became its first female officer. Shirley was elected AAAD's secretary-treasurer during the AAAD's National Basketball Tournament in Boston, Massachusetts in 1988. She is the first woman to become an officer in the AAAD's 43-year history.

Coast-To-Coast

Becky Bonheyo, Estella Bustamante and **Marsha Wetzel** spent the summer of 1986 crossing the country on bicycles.

Favorite stop — Laramie, Wyoming. They went to a bike shop to fix Marsha's bike and the owner invited them home for dinner, serving lasagna, beer and champagne with blueberry crepes for dessert. They stayed the night and woke to pancakes with blueberries.

Least favorite stop — Austine Junctionville, Oregon, a town that consisted of one building with a gas station, a grocery, a 3x8-foot post office. They would have slept outside, but it looked like rain, so they asked for a place to sleep. The owner waved them toward the post office. *"We were packed in like sardines,"* Estella said, adding that the rain never came.

Best acting job — at a truck stop off the highway in Wythesville, Virginia with six rooms for truckers only and nowhere else to sleep. *"Act sick,"* Estella signed to Marsha who laid her head on her arms. They got a room.

Oddest greeting — from a hand-made dummy clutching a handker-

Third from left: Carol Billone, Vice Chairwoman of the XV World Games for the Deaf at Los Angeles. Photo by David Cherkis.

chief outside a house in Missouri. As the cyclists rode by, a woman came out of the house and pulled a rope which caused the dummy to wave the handkerchief.

Becky, Estella and Marsha covered 4,000 miles from Florence, Oregon to Yorktown, Virginia with only $2,000 between them. They cycled through Oregon, Idaho, Wyoming, Colorado, Kansas, Missouri, Illinois, Kentucky, and Virginia.

World Games for the Deaf

Stacia Barron, Betsy Bachtel and Donalda Ammons were three deaf women with the group that invited President Ronald Reagan to be the Honorary Chairman of the World Games for the Deaf in 1985. He accepted.

Stacia Barron coaching at Model Secondary School. Gallaudet Photo Lab.

Milan, Italy, in 1957, was the site where Marie Kamuchey Smith and Sally Herran Maxwell were the first American deaf women to participate in WGD swimming events.

In 1969, California's Kathleen Russell was the captain of the first U.S. volleyball team to play in the WGD.

Gwen Rocque, of New York, was the flag-bearer for the USA delegates at the 1977 WGD. She

has amassed a total of eight medals in tennis (four gold, two silver, two bronze) at the 1965, '73 and '77 WGD. She was only 16 years old when she started participating in these events.

Sharon Ann Dror, figure skater and native of Santa Monica, California, participated in WGD 1975 Winter Games Sports. She won many awards and championships and was named to 1978 NBC Junior Hall of Fame.

Nancy Bonura, born to deaf family skiers, was the only American skier to win two third-place medals and one fourth-place medal at the age of 13 at the 1977 WGD in West Germany. She also participated in the Deaf Olympics at Lake Placid, New York, in 1975. Working at a filling station to earn money for her trip to the International Skiing Competition in the 9th Winter Games for the Deaf in France was in fruition. Nancy was one of the eight profiles in *"Successful Deaf Americans"* by Darlene K. Toole.

Laurie Barber won 10 gold medals in swimming at the 1977 WGD in Bucharest, Romania.

Stacia Barron, an Iowan basketball player, was invited to the White House for her team's accomplishment—winning the gold medal from the XIV World Games for the Deaf in Germany.

"Eating European meals was an experience," writes **Eva S. Kruger**, WGD chaperone. *"While in Cologne, Germany, I went to a beautiful German restaurant. Unfortunately, the menu was all in German. I hunted for a word for soup. Then I saw a waitress bringing a bowl of soup to a man at the next table and I told my waitress that I wanted that soup.*

"I got it and it was so, so delicious, I asked her to point to the name of the soup on the menu. To my surprise it was the longest word on the menu.

"A few days later," Eva continued, *"I went to the same restaurant again. The same waitress handed the menu to me. I noticed the longest word that was easy for me to remember so I ordered the soup by pointing to it on the menu. The waitress responded with a nice, big smile. No need for me to learn the German language."*

Vicki Kitsembel Grossinger of Arizona, former WGD volleyball player, was appointed the first USA Deaf Team Director for the American Deaf Volleyball Assn. (ADVBA). Her responsibilities include overseeing all aspects of development for both women's and men's programs.

Vicki recalled her experience playing volleyball in Romania in 1977. The gym had a very unusual greenish-colored floor. When she practiced her moves like diving at the floor, her clothes and kneepads

Vicki Kitsembel-Grossinger, a three-time World Games Volleyball player, won her first gold medal beating Denmark—1985. Photo by Richard J. Schoenberg.

turned green. The team settled for a silver medal.

In 1987, family and friends collected money to send **Kelly Schemenauer**, a Michigan gymnast, to Russia to study their gymnastic program for youngsters.

American Athletic Association of the Deaf—AAAD

At Los Angeles in 1964, **Lillian Hahn Skinner** was the first Chairwoman of an AAAD Basketball Tournament. **Ann Garretson Benedict** followed as the second chairwoman of an AAAD Tourney in 1965 in Cincinnati.

Ann Garretson Benedict, a product of the Central Institute for the Deaf, needed an ASL interpreter during the 1965 AAAD Basketball Tournament in Cincinnati. She was the general chairwoman and she had no problems in getting things organized for this big event. The deaf community was very cooperative and helped in every way possible. The problem was the *"ASL multitudes who invaded the city like a plague."*

Helen Thomas, an expert in skeet shooting, was named the first Deaf Athlete-of-the-Year by AAAD in 1955. Deaf since birth, 15-year-old Helen became the youngest national trapshooting champion

Helen C. Thomas—North American Women's Clay Target Trap Shooting champion.

in the history of the North America Women's Clay Target in 1955. She shot down 197 out of 200 clay birds. She was from Los Angeles, California. She was named in the 1987 Hall of Fame.

In 1959, **Gillian Hall** of Bristol, Connecticut, was the AAAD Athlete-of-the-Year for her accomplishments as an outstanding synchronized swimming star.

Rita Windbrake from the Federal Republic of Germany (West Germany) was named Deaf Athlete-of-the-Century at the Hall of Fame luncheon in San Francisco in 1983.

Through the efforts of **Donalda Ammons** in 1987, the USA Deaf Wrestling Team competed in Moscow—the first International Deaf Wrestling Tournament in six years. All expenses except for transportation between USA and

Donalda K. Ammons, first vice-chairwoman of the USA World Games, 1982–1986. Gallaudet Photo Lab.

Russia were paid by the Russian Federation of Deaf Sports.

Donalda's involvement with WGD began in 1980 when she served as a Spanish translator for the U.S. Soccer Team that went to Mexico City.

"My first name is DONALDA," she writes. *"I am often being assigned to share a hotel room with a male, or being addressed as the head of the household by advertising solicitors, or receiving mail order booklets from male clothiers.*

"Back in 1974 I was elected as the first female Editor-in-Chief of the Tower Clock yearbook in the history of Gallaudet. So when I received a new batch of letterheads for the Tower Clock," grimaces Donalda, *"I was not surprised to find my name printed as Donald K. Ammons."* Donalda, a native Marylander, was the youngest recipient of the dedication of a Tower Clock Yearbook—in 1980.

"The first time ever that the AAAD appointed a female as an officer of a standing committee,"

Ammons concludes, *"I was the Vice Chairwoman of the USA-World Games 1982-86. This was never an easy task when trying to make a point to the die-hard male members."*

Agnes Dunn Sutcliffe, the Gallaudet's second physical education instructor, managed to juggle her time between two careers: raising five children and as a professor. She was an all-round athlete at the Nebraska School for the Deaf in Omaha.

Agnes Dunn Sutcliffe

During the Gallaudet years, she was elected captain of the volleyball and field hockey teams, and was a high scorer in basketball. In 1958 she also held three high offices: President of the Women's Athletic Association, editor of women's sports for the *Buff and Blue,* and editor of women's sports for the 1959 yearbook, *The Tower Clock.* She now coordinates the Family Sign Language Program.

Ruth Taubert Seeger from Minnesota was the first American deaf woman to participate in track and field events in the World Games held in Milan, Italy, in 1957.

She was also the first deaf woman to be selected for the AAAD Hall of Fame in 1975.

Throughout Ruth's coaching career, many of her Texas students have won medals at the WGD as well as at local track and field meets in Texas. Her charges have also accumulated a total of 27 medals at the WGD from 1967 through 1985. (At the age of 15, Suzy Barker, a hurdler/sprinter from Texas won four medals at the WGD in 1969.)

"I will never forget," says Ruth, *"the afternoon Ray Butler called me into his office. He was head of the Physical Education Department at the Texas School and asked me what I thought about entering the 1957 WGD to be held in Milan, Italy.*

"I exclaimed, 'What! Me in the Games! Oh no. Not at my age.' I was then about to turn 33 in a few weeks and I had not known there was a women's track and field competition.

"Ray reminded me of what I did when I was little—how I used to run and jump and even pole vault, trying to be like Babe Didrickson," Ruth continued. *"I hit 4' 4" in the high jump (2" shy of the world record). Ray thought that might get me a place on the U.S. team."*

At Ruth's retirement in May, 1986, Governor Mark White issued a proclamation recognizing her as an Honorary Texan.

During the Homecoming Game in October, 1987, the South Campus gymnasium at the Texas School was named the Ruth Taubert Seeger Gymnasium in

Ruth Taubert Seeger

honor of Ruth's many years of service and outstanding contributions to the deaf in sports.

"When I started teaching in 1949," Ruth recalls, *"I was only going to work for one year. Then I was going to quit and become a housewife. But I kept putting it off until 1986 when I finally retired.*

"It felt good to be the first American deaf woman to participate in the World Games. I was frustrated at that time, too, because I did not have a coach. The other coaches were busy with the men."

Daredevils

Jan DeLap, the daughter of a motorcycle cop in Delavan, Wisconsin, grew up with motorcycles. Her former husband, the originator of the *Globe of Death* show, was a traveling daredevil motorcyclist in the 1960's. Jan and her husband rode their motorcycles, doing their

loop-the-loop tricks which excited the crowds.

She once mentioned that she felt more afraid of riding in traffic than when she rode in the carnivals in their steel Globe.

Former circus daredevil Jan eventually settled in the D.C. area and works in the composing room

Jan DeLap

Kitty O'Neil

of the Washington Post. She has become an active member of the deaf community. Jan took part in the annual Smithsonian Institution's Festival of American Folklife. This show is called *Deaf Kaleidoscope* where hearing audiences learn about deafness.

Kitty O'Neill, one of the world's greatest stuntwomen stands 5'3½" tall and weighs 97 pounds. She once drove a car powered by a 48,000 horsepower rocket motor at 618 miles per hour. In swimming as a diver, Kitty won several National AAU championships.

She participated for the United States at the 1964 Tokyo Olympics.

"I want to help handicapped people," stated the Hollywood stuntwoman. *"I want them to remember that they can do anything. You can't give up. You have to meet the challenge."*

The 1921 California Motor Vehicle Code contained a clause providing for a physical examination by all licensed drivers as to sight and hearing. This angered Mrs. Walter Eden, deaf wife of a state senator, who drove her husband to and from the State Capital.

Mrs. Eden invited a deaf friend, Miss Warren, to join her in giving legislators a practical demonstration to show how good a deaf driver can be.

The result was the removal of the word "hearing" from the act. Not lulled by her victory, she warned deaf drivers that their privilege to drive was only temporary until the next session of the legislature.

The same thing happened all over the country. Deaf people had to fight to prove that they are safe drivers.

There is no record of who was the first deaf women driver, but **Mrs. B. L. Winston** had a Scripps-Booth and **Miss Leona G. Morden** had two Cadillacs. Both ladies from Minneapolis, Minnesota, were considered very skillful and careful drivers in the 1920's.

Pilots

Deaf-mutes are not the only ones who talk without words. Aviators are the latest to develop this means of communication because of the incessant noise of the engine. Unable to make themselves heard otherwise, they have invented a sign language.
— *The Silent Worker,* 1920

Rebecca Ann Center, of Ohio, deaf since birth, passed her Federal Aviation Administration flight examination in December 1986. The only exception to the license is that it restricts her from using larger airports where radio communication is required.

She communicates with light signals and requests clearance for take-off by clicking her microphone switch. Controllers flash a green light beam if the plane is cleared to proceed; red if it is not.

Rebecca fell in love with flying when as a youngster she took a light plane ride. She was again inspired when the family visited Kitty Hawk, North Carolina, where the Wright Brothers made their flight.

South Dakota's **Nellie Zabel Willhite**, the first female pilot, was a barnstormer in her home state. She was licensed in 1928 and was a charter member of the Ninety-Nines of which Amelia Earhart was a member.

The plane PARD, a gift from her father, was used in air shows throughout the Midwest. The original propeller is in the Taylor Museum, Hill City, South Dakota.

"Roy and I taught at the South Dakota School in Sioux Falls for eight years, 1947–55," marvels **Mabs Holcomb**. *"We made many trips to the Black Hills during those years but were not aware of Nellie's accomplishments. Nor were we aware the propeller of her plane was displayed there. That was a shame."*

According to *Deaf Heritage* by Jack Gannon, **Allie Joiner**, **Margaret Leitch**, and **Nellie Zabel Willhite** were the first three deaf women to have earned a pilot's license. Later **Jean Hauser** got hers in Wisconsin in 1965, and Rebecca A. Center, in Ohio, in 1987.

As of 1988 among the 1,700 hearing impaired pilots in the United States is **Jean Hauser**. She, over 30 years an assembler at Auto Lock, was the first person to get her pilot's license in Wisconsin in 1967. Jean took her first flying lessons from the two instructors who communicated with her using pencil and pad. Jean asks her hearing friend to help with the use of the radio equipment on long trips.

Nellie Zabel Willhite with "PARD"–1928. Reprint from **Deaf Heritage** *— Rise Studio.*

After notifying the control tower of her deafness, in her solo flight, she watches for the light signals for takeoffs and landings.

She is in Darlene Toole's *"Courageous Deaf Adults"* displaying courageous effort in achieving excellence in her avocation. *"My deafness sometimes bothers me,"* reports Jean, *"but I do not feel that I have a handicap. I live a very exciting life and feel very lucky."*

"I can still remember the day vividly," says **Allie Joiner** of Seattle. *"I was frustrated with my instructor who would write notes to me as we were flying a Cessna during my lessons. He saw a friend of mine at the terminal so he got her to cuss me out in sign language.*

"I walked back to the Cessna fuming, went through the motions up there in the sky, when he signaled me to go down. I thought, 'Oh, no, I was going to get another bawling out.' Taxiing toward the terminal, he said for me to hit the brakes. Quickly he got out, saying 'Go!'

"I was excited!! Anxious!! What, me go alone? Wheee!" Allie remembered. *"I went up—up—up! The exhilaration of my first solo flight will never be equalled again."*

The basketball squad on a winning streak at Gallaudet, circa 1920. Courtesy of Gallaudet Archives.

The basketball team at Gallaudet—1898. Courtesy of Gallaudet Archives.

DEAF WOMEN

*The first women's athletic team in "Ole Jim"—
1896. The site was the scene of a large meeting
of the Suffragette Movement on March 3, 1913.
Courtesy of Gallaudet Archives.*

Top: The Girls' Athletic Association at California School for the Deaf at Berkeley, circa 1945.

Above: After the game's party at Ohio School for the Deaf—1940's.

Left: Lorraine "Polly" Brady, Cheerleader, at the Arizona School for the Deaf—1961.

Tailpiece

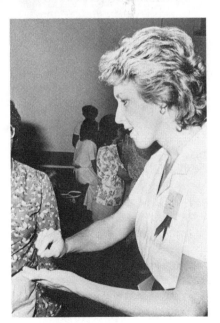

AUTHORS

Mabs Holcomb

Retiree/Author
Fremont, California and
Rochester, New York

Marjoriebell Stakley Holcomb, known as "Mabs," is a product of the Ohio School for the Deaf and is a member of the Gallaudet College (University) class of 1947. She has earned two Master's Degrees: one from the University of Tennessee (1957) and the second from California State University at Northridge—National Leadership Training Program (1968).

Along with her husband, Roy Kay Holcomb, Mabs has taught at several schools around the country: South Dakota, Tennessee and Indiana. She finally broke out of the mold, going into a California public school in Santa Ana and later, doing her bit in post-secondary instruction of the deaf at Golden West College, Huntington Beach, California.

Mabs followed Roy to Delaware in 1974, a year after he had accepted the offer to direct Margaret S. Sterck School for the Hearing Impaired in Newark, Delaware.

While living in Delaware, Mabs was in charge of the state-wide Deaf-Blind Search Program.

Roy and Mabs moved back to California in 1977. She taught at Ohlone College in Fremont, California for a long time. Later, she had the reins of the federally supported Regional Interpreter Train-

Marjoriebell Stakley Holcomb. Photo Credit: Chun Louie.

ing Program serving California, Nevada, Arizona and Utah.

Before health problems forced Mabs into early retirement, she was the director of the Gallaudet University Regional Center based at Ohlone College.

Mabs assisted Roy in many of

his well-known innovative contributions to the education of the deaf over the past 40 years.

Her deaf sons, Sam and Tom, and three grand-daughters, Tara, Amy and Leala are the great pride and joy of her life.

Mabs cherishes the love of her family and her friends from all walks of life.

DEAF WOMEN

Sharon Kay Wood

Instructor
Entertainer/Lecturer
 Hyattsville, Maryland

Sharon Kay Wood (Pisces) was born in Idaho. Her parents, Jo Ann and Ray King Wood, who were educators, spent 20 years working with Indian tribes on reservations, hence, she attended state schools for the deaf in Washington, Idaho, Iowa, and finally was graduated with honors from the Arizona School and Gallaudet College (University) in 1968.

Sharon's first love has always been acting. At Gallaudet, she earned both "Best Supporting Actress" and "Most Promising Actress" awards. She was formerly with the Spectrum Focus on Deaf Artists Theatre in Texas, the New York (City) Deaf Theatre and the National Theatre of the Deaf.

Sharon took post-graduate courses at New York University for her teaching certificate and master's degree. She has 20 years' teaching experience at schools for the deaf, in Rome, NY.; South Carolina; Texas; and Wayne, NJ. Currently, her teaching duties are

Sharon Kay Wood. Photo Credit: J. L. Cartledge.

with the Kendall Demonstration Elementary School — Middle School in Washington, D.C.

On weekends and during summer months, Sharon goes on the road conducting one-woman shows and workshops relating to issues of deaf women. She is the third chairwoman of the Deaf Women Section of the NAD (1986–88). She writes a column in the NAD newspaper entitled "Women At Work."

Her leisure time is spent raising Boston terriers, collecting antiques, traveling, attending plays and in spiritual growth.

by Margaret Myhre, San Francisco Public Library

BIBLIOGRAPHY

"Access to Equality: The First Conference on Education Equity for Deaf Women." Laura-Jean Gilbert. *Deaf American* Vol. 35, #4, 1983. Pp. 17–18. A report on a June 1983 conference which brought together disabled women, educators and people in the field of civil rights for a discussion of the problems faced by disabled women and possible strategies to solve these problems.

"Being Deaf . . . Being a Woman." *Gallaudet Today.* Vol 4, #4. (Spring, 1974). Pp. 6–11. The results of a survey, conducted by *Gallaudet Today,* in which 51 deaf women from across the United States respond to questions on deafness and attitudes toward women.

"Betty Broecker: Community Service Worker." Ruth Brown. *The Deaf American.* April, 1976. Pp. 7–9. Betty Broecker, who began losing her hearing at the age of 5, is the coordinator of the Community Service Center for the Deaf in Philadelphia. She is a divorced mother of four children.

California Association of the Deaf: A History 1906–1982. Emil S. Ladner, Bill White and Barbara Wild. Sacramento, California: California Association of the Deaf, 1983. Pp. 6-10. Information about CAD's three women presidents: Alice T. Terry (1923–1926), Isabel M. Lester (1927–1931), and Lillian Skinner (1975–1977).

"Can a Woman? Deaf Kids Respond." Nancy Kelly-Jones. *Gallaudet Today.* Vol. 14, #4 (Summer, 1984). Pp. 9–11. Results of a survey given to 61 females and 35 males between the ages of 10 and 21. All are hearing impaired students. They were asked to study a list of 35 job titles and indicate whether a woman could handle the perceived responsibilities of the job.

"Cheryl Kent . . . Advocate for Handicapped Individuals." Nancy Conners. *Gallaudet Today.* Vol. 14, #4 (Summer, 1984). Pp. 22–23. Cheryl Kent is a Civil Rights Specialist with the U.S. Department of Housing and Urban Development's office of Fair Housing and Equal Opportunity. She is a 1978 graduate of Gallaudet.

"Comparison of Sex-Role Attitudes of Hearing and Hearing Impaired Women." Susan Anderson and Albert Krueger. *Journal of Rehabilitation of the Deaf.* Vol. 1, #2 (October, 1982). Pp. 1–4.

"Cultural Arts Among Deaf People." Robert Panara. Gallaudet Today. Vol. 13, #3 (Spring, 1983). Pp. 12–16. An overview of the cultural achievements of members of the Deaf Community including Linda Bove (actress), Phyllis Frelich (actress), Jane Wilk (actress and newsperson), Frances Woods (dancer), Kitty O'Neil (stuntwoman) and other deaf women artists.

"Deaf and Gay: Where is My Community?" Charles N. Barthell. *Networking and Deafness.* Silver Spring, Maryland: American Deafness and Rehabilitation Association, 1983. A discussion of the growing link between the deaf/gay community and the hearing/gay community. The author suggests that a number of common bonds of experience contribute to this alliance. According to a study cited by the author, there are approximately 12,690 deaf lesbian women in the U.S.

"The Deaf Woman." Nancy Rarus. *I'm Deaf Too: Twelve Deaf Americans.* Silver Spring, Maryland: National Association of the Deaf, 1973. Pp. 28–33. An interview with Nancy Rarus, a deaf teacher at the American School for the Deaf in Connecticut, who discusses her feelings about the woman's movement and deaf women.

"The Deaf Woman as Wife and Mother: Two Views." Ruth Peterson and JoAnn Pelarski. *Gallaudet Today.* Vol. 4, #3 (Spring, 1974). Pp. 20–23. Two deaf women discuss their childhoods, their educations, their family lives, and their views on deaf people in a hearing world.

"Deaf Women — A Double Handicap in Career Development." Laurian Kovulchik and Judy E.

DEAF WOMEN

Dudd. *Social Science Record.* 12 (Spring, 1975). Pp. 25–26. A discussion of how deafness and gender can create a double handicap in the areas of career development and employment.

"Deaf Women and the Women's Movement." *The Deaf American* 29 (April, 1977). Pp. 10–11. A discussion of the women of the Deaf Community and their role in the women's movement.

"Deaf Women: We Were There Too!" Roslyn Rosen, Ed.D. *The Deaf American.* Vol. 36, #3. (1984). Pp. 4–9. A survey of the vital roles that deaf women of America have had, and continue to have, in the making of the history and the future of deaf people everywhere.

"Deafness and Deaf Women." Mary Anne Pugin. *Off Our Backs.* Vol. XI, #5 (May, 1981). Pp. 31. A deaf woman discusses her experiences growing up, in school and as a deaf lesbian.

"Donalda Ammons . . . Vice Chairman of USWGD Committee." Patricia Cinelli. *Gallaudet Today.* Vol. 14, #4 (Summer, 1984). Pp. 25–26 Donalda Ammons, a doctoral student at Gallaudet College, is vice chairman of the U.S. Committee for the World Games for the Deaf. She is the first woman to ever serve on this committee.

"The First National Deaf Women's Conference." JoAnne Brinninstool. *Gallaudet Today.* Vol. 6, #3 (Spring, 1976). Pp. 1–7. A participant in the conference describes the proceedings of the meeting and lists the priorities which were identified by the delegates.

The Gallaudet Almanac. Jack R. Gannon, editor. Washington, D.C.: Gallaudet College Alumni Association, 1974. In addition to the information about Gallaudet students who excelled athletically or academically, the almanac has information about officers in Gallaudet's three sororities: Chi Omega Psi (1970), Delta Epsilon (1953) and Phi Kappa Zeta (1892).

"Guest Editoral: We, the Outsiders . . ." Gertrude Scott Galloway. *Gallaudet Today.* Vol. 14, #4 (Summer, 1984). Pp. 6–7. Gertrude Scott Galloway was the first woman to serve as president of the National Association of the Deaf. She believes deaf women are outsiders because they are now challenging the traditional concepts of their roles as deaf women. Deaf women need to speak out to help foster equal opportunity and more humane environments for everyone.

"Happy Warriors." William J.A. Marshall. *Gallaudet Today.* Vol. 14, #4 (Summer, 1984). Pp. 28–32. Dr. William Marshall, a hearing impaired professor in the School of Education and Human Services at Gallaudet, discusses women in management. Most women managers feel that they need to exhibit a greater competency and measure up to more stringent criteria than is required by their male counterparts.

Image of Ourselves: Women With Disabilities Talking. Jo Campling, editor. London: Routledge and Kegan Paul, 1981. Pp. 33–38. A collection of short essays by disabled women of all ages, backgrounds and from all parts of the United Kingdom. Maggie, a woman who became deaf at the age of 16, describes her experiences in accepting her deafness and her efforts to make her hearing peers accept her on equal terms. She is a single parent with two hearing daughters.

"Influence of Sexism on the Education of Handicapped Children." Patricia H. Gillespie and Albert H. Fink. *Exceptional Children.* November, 1974. Pp. 155–162. The identification of exceptional children as either male or female results in arbitrary practice, discriminatory judgments and decisions with limit opportunities for personal and vocational development.

"The Intellect of Women." Agatha M. Tiegel. *Gallaudet Today.* Vol. 4, #3 (Spring, 1974). Pp. 1–3. Agatha M. Tiegel, a 1893 graduate of Gallaudet College, presented this speech at Presentation Day Exercises on April 26, 1893. Her topic is that people are accustomed to seeing women at a stage of development so far below her actual potential that they assume women are intellectually inferior. Women are actually the victims of restrictive circumstances. Poems by the author are included.

"The Invisible Isolation of Deaf Women: Its Effect on Social Awareness." Gaylene Becker and Joanne Jauregui. *Journal of Sociology and Social Welfare.* Vol. VIII, #2. (July, 1981). The place of deaf women in relation to society is discussed. Deaf women's needs are outlined and suggestions are made to providers to meet these needs.

"Julia Burg Mayes . . . A Deaf Woman Serving Others." Laura-Jean Gilbert. *Gallaudet Today.* Vol. 14, #4 (Summer, 1984). Pp. 20–22. A biographical profile of Julia Burg Mayes, volunteer with the Gallaudet Visitors' Center Program and with the National Health Care Foundation for the Deaf. A 1944 graduate of Gallaudet, Julia and her twin sister, Celia were born deaf. Julia has served as National President of Phi Kappa Zeta and Celia was the Quota Club's Woman of the Year in 1979.

"Linda Risser Lytle. . .Mother, Wife, Counselor and Student." Mike Kaika. *Gallaudet Today.* Vol. 14, #4 (Summer, 1984). Pp. 24–26. Linda Lytle is a school psychologist at the Model Secondary School for the Deaf. She is also an intern in clinical psychology at St. Elizabeth's Mental Health Program for the Deaf and a mother of four year old daughter.

"Mental Health Needs of the Deaf Woman." Roslyn Rosen, Ed.D. *Mental Health in Deafness.* Experimental Issue I (Fall, 1977). Pp. 82–84. A discussion of the training needs of deaf women including assertiveness training, awareness of legal rights, sex education, career exploration, consumer education, and training in dealing with hearing people and agencies.

"Michelle Craig Smithdas: Deaf-Blind Bride." Ruth Brown. *The Deaf American.* December, 1976. Pp 27–29. A biographical portrait of a woman who was born with a hearing loss and gradually lost her vision after a serious snowmobile accident during her senior year at Gallaudet College.

"Minnesota's First Deaf Women's Conference." Linda Kessler Nelson. *The Deaf American.* Vol.31,

#5 (1979). Pp. 15–16. A report on the conference which was held on June 3, 1978 in Bloomington, Minnesota. The conference was inspired by the National Deaf Women's Conference which was held in Washington, D.C. in 1976.

"Nansie Sharpless." *Comeback: Six Remarkable People Who Triumphed Over Disability.* Frank Bowe, editor. New York: Harper and Row, 1980. Pp. 127–149. Nansie Sharpless is a scientist who is doing research on the brain at Albert Einstein College of Medicine in New York. She became deaf from meningitis as a high school freshman. She discusses how being a woman, deaf and a Quaker has affected her life.

"No More Stares." Conceived and developed by Ann Cupolo Carrillo, Katherine Corbett and Victoria Lewis. Berkeley, California: Disability Rights, Education and Defense Fund, 1982. Disabled women discuss their lives including such areas as self-image, school, relationships, work and parenting. Deaf contributors include Lois Dadzie, Susan Vaccaro and Joanne Jauregui. Excellent resource guide at the back of the book.

"Occupational Prestige and Its Correlates as Conceived by Deaf Female Vocational Students." Daryl Duprez. *American Annals of the Deaf.* 116 (August, 1971). Pp. 408–412. A study of 30 deaf female vocational students and the variables which contribute to occupational prestige, the role of parents and peers in prestige formation, and awareness of available occupations.

"On the Accomplishments of Some Deaf Men and Women." Francis C. Higgins. Riverside, California: California School for the Deaf, Junior National Association of the Deaf Chapter, 1965. Pp. 12–19. Professor Higgins lists the accomplishments of several deaf women including a deaf court stenographer, a nurse, the 1955 winner of the Women's Clay Target Championships, a medical researcher, artists, dancers, writers and poets.

"Overcoming Occupational Stereotypes related to Sex and Deafness." Judy E. Dudd. *American Annals of the Deaf.* October, 1977. Pp. 489–491. Summer Vestible students at the National Technical Institute for the Deaf were asked to rate jobs as appropriate for women only, men only, hearing only, etc. The data gathered offers feedback for the revision of career planning programs.

"Reflections of Five Deaf Women." *Gallaudet Today.* Vol. 14, #4 (Summer, 1984). Pp. 1–4. Five deaf women including Jean Kelsch Cordano, Astrid Goodstein, Dorothy S. Miles, Helen E. Muse and Bettie Spellman discuss the changes they perceive to have occurred for deaf women between 1974 and 1984.

"Ruth T. Seeger: Sportswoman And Coach." Pattie Cinelli. *Gallaudet Today.* Vol. 14, #4 (Summer, 1984). Pp. 26–27. An interview with Ruth T. Seeger, physical education teacher and coach at the Texas School for the Deaf, and the first American woman to compete in the women's track and field division of the World Games for the Deaf.

"The Sex Role Attitudes of Deaf Adolescent Women and Their Implications for Vocational Choice." Linda Cook and Allision Rosenstein. *American Annals of the Deaf.* 120 (June, 1975). Pp. 341–345. In this study, the sex role attitudes of hearing and deaf women were compared. Deaf women were found to have more traditional perceptions of sex role attitudes. The implications of sex role perceptions as they influence vocational choice are discussed.

"She Knows By Your Hands." Dolores Follette as told to Elinore Worflus. *Off Our Backs.* Vol. XI, #5 (May, 1981). Pp. 16–17 & 30. Dolores (Dee) Follette lost her sight at the age of two years and six months, and lost her hearing at the age of ten. She describes her experiences as a wife, mother, student and as a deaf-blind person.

"Socio-Economic Status of Deaf Women: Are They Disadvantages?" Sharon N. Barnartt. Manuscript. 198? 27 pages. This paper asks if deaf women are doubly disadvantaged in the way that other minority women are — if they have lower socio-economic status than both hearing women and deaf men. It uses the 1972 National Census of the Deaf Population and comparable national statistics for the hearing population.

"Vocational Status and Adjustment of Women." Leo Connor and Joseph Rosenstein. *Volta Review* 65 (December, 1963). Pp 585–591. A study of 177 deaf female graduates of Lexington School for the Deaf. These women were asked to complete a survey, as a result the authors conclude that vocational programs for the deaf girls need to be reviewed and attuned to modern technology.

What Happens After School? A Study of Disabled Women and Education. Women's Educational Equity Communications Network, Far West Laboratory, San Francisco, California. 1978 (ERIC Document # ED166894). Women representing several disabled groups discuss their early family and school experiences, high school and work situations. Joanne Jauregui describes her experiences as a deaf woman.

Women and Deafness compiled by Margaret Myhre. San Francisco Main Library, Civic Center, San Francisco, California. May, 1984.

Where are Our Deaf Women? Nancy Kelly-Jones. *Gallaudet Today.* Vol. 4, #3 (Spring, 1974). Pp. 24–29. A demographic analysis of the attitudes, majors, goals and occupations of female graduates of Gallaudet College from 1971 to 1973.

"Women are Too Emotional." Barbara P. Harslem. *Gallaudet Today.* Vol. 4, #4 (Spring, 1974). Pp. 30–33. Eight deaf female graduate students in education and counseling at Gallaudet College reflect on the impact of sex role stereotypes have had on their school and home experiences as well as on their general development.

"Women in the Deaf Community." Edna Adler. *Gallaudet Today.* Vol. 4, #3 (Spring, 1974). A guest editorial for *Gallaudet Today* in which Edna Adler emphasizes the need for positive role models for deaf girls who need to develop a better self-image. They need to know that there is room in the world for deaf heroines.

Films and Videotapes

Choices. Gallaudet College Media Center. VHS videocassette. 28 minutes. Color. 1978. Signed/sound. A dramatic presentation of two couples (one deaf and one hearing) who are involved in major decisions that will affect their lifestyles and their families. One couple must decide on whether to buy a home or not, while the second couple's dilemma revolves around the difficulties of a working mother.

Deaf Minorities. San Francisco Public Library. 30 minutes. Color. 1984. Signed/closed captioned. Several Bay Area deaf women who are members of racial and cultural minority groups within the Deaf Community appear in this program. Donnette Reins, Lois Dadzie, Marta Ordaz and Rosemary Ortiz present their perceptions of women in the Deaf Community.

Deaf Women: Ambitious Dreams, Emerging Dreams. National Technical Institute for the Deaf, 29 minutes. Color. 1979. Captioned. A documentary which presents two contemporary deaf women who meet life's challenges at home, at work and in the community. The women describe their roles in these settings, why they chose such roles and their plans for the future.

The Death of Minnehaha. National Association of the Deaf. 16 minutes. Black and White. 1913. Silent/signed. This film which is a part of the

George Veditz Historic film Collection at Gallaudet College, shows Mary Williamson presenting Longfellow's poem, "The Death of Minnehaha," in American Sign Language. This is probably the oldest existing film of a deaf woman performer. A portion of the film can be seen in the videotape "Our Most Priceless Gift," which is available at the San Francisco Public Library.

"Going Past Go." Essay on sexism. VHS videocassette. 60 minutes. Color. 1980. Captioned/sound. A documentary on sexism, offering definitions of the word and examples of how it affects men and women in social, political and economic areas of society. Sexism in school textbooks and stereotypes placed on children in early stages of development are discussed. Statistics on earning power of men and women are presented. Available from the San Francisco Public Library.

Red House. Boston Shakespeare Company and Theatre Access for the Deaf. 20 minutes. Color. 1983. Captioned. A portrait of a community residence for deaf women who have been diagnosed as having emotional and behavioral problems. Winner of "Outstanding Contribution" award from the North Shore Association for Retarded Citizens.

See What I Say. Linda Chapman, Pam LeBlanc and Freddi Stevens. 24 minutes. Color. 1981. Captioned/particlly signed. Feminist folksinger Holly Near is featured in this program with her sign language interpreter, Susan Freundlich. Included in the program are the experiences of four deaf women. Nominated for an Academy Award. Distributed by Filmmakers Library.

Sign of Victory. Marshall Grupp. 22 minutes. Color. 1980. No captions. A sports documentary about a high school basketball team for deaf girls. One of the girls, Maria communicates in American Sign Language while her parents can only communicate in Spanish. The loneliness Maria feels at home disappears on the basketball court. Filmed at the Rhode Island School for the Deaf. Distributed by Filmmakers Library.

Acronyms Used in the Book

AAAD	American Athletic Association of the Deaf
AARP	American Association of Retired Persons
AGB	Alexander Graham Bell Association
ASD	American School for the Deaf, Hartford, Connecticut
ASL	American Sign Language
BDA	Black Deaf Advocates
CSUN	California State University at Northridge
DAA	Deaf Artists of America
DCARA	Deaf Counseling Advocacy and Referral Agency
DP	Deaf Pride
DWU	Deaf Women United
GAN	Gallaudet Alumni Newsletter
GLAD	Greater Los Angeles Council on Deafness, Inc.
GUAA	Gallaudet University Alumni Association
ITU	International Typographical Union
Jr.NAD	Junior National Association of the Deaf
KDES	Kendall Demonstration Elementary School
MSSD	Model Secondary School for the Deaf
NAD	National Association of the Deaf
NCI	National Captioning Institute
NFSD	National Fraternal Society
NLTP	National Leadership Training Program
NSC	NTID Student Congress
NTD	National Theatre of the Deaf
NTID	National Technical Institute for the Deaf
ODAS	Oral Deaf Adult Section W/AGB
PKZ	Phi Kappa Zeta
RID	Registry of Interpreters for the Deaf
RIT	Rochester Institute of Technology
RSC	Reverse Skills Certificate
SBG	Student Body Government
SEE-2	Signing Exact English
WGD	World Games for the Deaf

INDEX

Abbreviations

Ack	Acknowledgment
Agenc	Agencies
Art	Art
Art Foto	Art Photography
Blkdeaf	Blackdeaf
Bus	Business World
CEd	Continuing Education
Children	Children of A Lesser God
Comm	Communication
CommSvc	Community Services
Dance	Dance
DD	Daredevils
DeafBlind	Deaf-Blind
Earlyear	Early Years
Ed	Education
Fed	Federal
Fem	Feminist
Foreword	Foreword
Gally	Deaf Women At Gallaudet
Honors	Honors
Intro	Introduction
Legal	Legal
Lib	Library
Lit	Literature
Mother	Mother
Movies	Movies
Music	Music
Org	Organization
Queen	Queens
Reli	Religion
Sports	Sports
Stage	Stage
TV	Television
Vict	Victorian Era

Name	Chapter	Name	Chapter
Barbee, Chris	Fem	Blumenthal, Betsy	Reli
Barbee, Lucy	Ed	Boardman, Elizabeth	Earlyear
Barber, Laurie	Sports	Boatner, E.	Earlyear
Barber, MaryBeth	TV, Lit, Queen	Bolling, Mary	Earlyear
Barker, Vivian	Mother	Boltz, Kathie	Lit
Barrett, Augusta	Ed	Bonheyo, Becky	Sports
Barron, Luanne	Mother	Bonheyo, Lori	Org, Bus
Barron, Maurice	Mother	Bonura, Nancy	Sports
Barron, Michelle	Reli	Booher, Reba	Bus
Barron, Stacia	Mother, Sports	Bounds-Wood, Betty	Ed
Bartee, Julie	Stage	Bourne, Bridgetta	Mother
Bartholick, Robin	Art	Bourne, Jenny Sue	Mother
Bartley, Joan	Med	Bove, Fannie	Bus
Bass, Barbara	Ed	Bove, Linda	Lit, Stage,
Batchel, Betsy	Sports	Boyd, Barbara	Ed
Battison, Robbin	Comm	Boyd, Mary B.	Lit
Beachman, Stephanie	TV	Brace, Julia	Earlyear
Bechera, Ellen	Stage	Braddock, G.	Earlyear, Lit
Becker, Gaylene	Lit	Brady, Lorraine Veronica	Sports
Becker, Nancy	CommSvc	Bragg, Bernard	Stage
Becker, June	Lit	Brandt, Alice	Reli, Mother
Bell, Alexander G.	Vict	Brasel, Barbara	Comm
Bell, Alexander M.	Vict	Brauer, Barbara	Ed
Bell, Mabel	Lit	Bravin, Jeff	Mother
Bellugi, Ursula	Comm	Bravin, Judith	Lit, Mother
Belsky, Marta	Lit	Breindel, Tina Jo	Ack, Lit
Benedict, Anne	Ed, Mother, Sports	Brennen, Patricia	Queen
Benensen, Esther	Reli, Org	Brenner, Dot	Bus
Bennett, Monica		Bridgeman, Laura	DeafBlind, Lit
Benoit, May	Med	Brightwell, Mary	CommSvc
Bentz, Betty	Org	Broecker, Elizabeth	CommSvc
Bergan, Stefan	Fem	Brooks, Diane	Blkdeaf
Bergman, Eugene	Stage	Brown, Katie	Blkdeaf, Ed, Lit
Berke, Joan	Legal, Org, Reli	Brown, Mary	Bus
Berke, Lilly	Stage	Brown, Mattie	Fem
Berke, Lisa	Bus	Brown, Ola	Stage, Ed
Berstein, Mary	Org	Buchholz, Christine	Fem, Org
Berzinsh, Henna	Lit	Budd, Elizabeth	Earlyear
Bethke, Virginia	Org	Bull, Beth Ann	Stage
Beverly, St John of	Reli	Burdick, Eulalia	Art
Bienvenu, Martina Jo	Comm	Burnes, Byron	Org
Billington, Ann	Lit, Queen	Burnes, Carolyn	Org
Billone, Carol	Stage, Honors	Bustamante, Estella	Sports, Stage
Birnum, Margaret	Org	Butler, Ray	Sports
Black, Ella	Earlyear, Comm	Buzzard, Henry	Ack, Earlyear
Blank, Jodi	Art		
Bloch, Nancy	Ed	Caldwell, Taylor	Lit
Bloomer, Amelia	Sports	Campbell, Agnes	Bus

Name	Chapter	Name	Chapter
Ewan, Darlene	Fem	Gold, Julianna	Stage
Ewan, Karl	Fem	Goldberg, Malvine	Reli
Ezzell, Teresa	Lit	Gompf, Allison	Stage
		Good, Margaret	Bus
Fabray, Nanette	Stage	Goodstein, Astrid	Fem
Fail, Geraldine	Lit	Goodstein, Harvey	Mother
Fay, E.A.	Lit	Gordon, Arthur	Vict
Feder, Susan	Ed	Gottlich, Lynn	Reli
Feld, Max	Reli	Gould, Sue	Stage
Feld-Gosman, Rose	Reli	Grace, Nora	Comm
Finklestein, Beverly	Reli	Granath, Stella	Reli
Finkle, Alrgail	Fem	Grant, Roslyn	Reli
Fischer, Angeline Fuller	Fem	Grappe, Susie	Bus
Fischer, Malvine	Lit	Green, Elizabeth	Ed
Fitzgerald, Edith	Ed	Greenberg, Joanne	TV
Fjeld, Julianna	Stage	Greene, Robin	Bus
Fleischman, Alexander	Ack	Gregory, Hester	Bus
Fleischman, Georgette	Ed	Grossinger, Vicki	Sports
Fletcher, Louise	Mother	Gustason, Gerilee	Ed
Follette, Dee	DeafBlind	Guttmagn, Anna	Reli
Font, Eleanor	Earlyear, Art, Lit		
Forman, Beth	Fem	Hagemeyer, Alice	Lit
Fouts, Sarah	CommSvc, Bus	Hainline, Eva	Bus
Fowler, Amy	Ed	Hall, Ethel	Vict
Fowler, Sophia	Earlyear	Hall, Gillian	Sports
Frelich, Esther	Mother	Hall, Harriet	Bus
Frelich, Phyllis	Children, Stage, Lit	Hall, Percival	Vict
French, Daniel	Art	Hall, Percival, Jr.	Vict
Frye, Sandra	Queen	Halvorson, Julie	Ed
		Hammons, Helen	Mother
Gallaudet, Edward	Earlyear, Lit	Hampton, Ida	Blkdef
Gallaudet, Rev. Thomas	Earlyear, Reli	Hanson, Agatha Tiegel	Intro, Earlyear, Fem, Org, Ed
Gallaudet, Thomas H.	Earlyear, Comm, Lit		
Galloway, Gertrude	Intro, Fem, Org, Ed	Hanson, Olaf	Earlyear
Gannon, Jack	Intro, Art, Sports	Harris, Rachel	Stage, Org, CommSrv
Gannon, Rosalyn	Art, Fem	Harris, Raychelle	Fem
Garretson, Carol	Lit	Harter, Carol	Ed
Garas, Joanne	Reli	Hartling, Virginia	Bus
Gemmill, Stephanie	Stage	Hathaway, Libby	Stage
Genderari, Cynthia	CommSvc	Hatrak, Marla	Bus
Genrich, Laura	Lit	Hauser, Jean	Sports
Giannoti, Judith	Ed	Havens, Dorothy	Org
Gibbons, Geraldine	Queen	Havens, Mary	Mother
Gilbert, James, Jr.	Blkdeaf	Hays, David	Stage
Gilliam, Judith	Ed	Heckman, Helen	Stage, Lit
Glassman, Shirley	Comm	Helberg, Lenore	Stage
Glennie, Evelyn	Stage	Herechak, Linda	Stage
Gold, Barbara	Reli	Hersom, Muriel	DeafBlind

Name	Chapter	Name	Chapter
Kubis, Shelby	Bus	Lynn, Loretta	Stage
Kuntze, Cindy	Comm	Lynn, Ollie	Bus
Kurtz, Anna	Earlyear	Lyon, Nancy	Vict
		Lytle, Linda	Ed, Fem
La Rue, Sandi	Blkdeaf, Lit		
Ladner, Mary	Ed	Mabry, Wayne	Fem
Laird, Wendy	CommSvc	Maddox, Helen	Med, Org
Lamarie, Dora	Med	Malzkuhn, Eric	Stage
Lampe, June	Honors	Malzkuhn, Mary	Ed
Lamson, Cloa	Org	Mantz, Rose	Stage
Lange, Camilla	Mother	Marbury, Nathie	Blkdeaf
Lange, Virginia	Ed	Marios, Marie	Art, Lit
Lashbrook, Annie	Org	Marloff, Frances	Queen
Larson, Caroline	Stage	Martin, Helen	DeafBlind
Larson, Herb	Stage	Martin, May	Earlyear
Laurenschlegar, Cinda	Ed	Martineau, Harriett	Fem
Lauritsen La, Reine	Lit	Martinez, Gloria	Ed
Lee, Barbara	Ed	Massey, Carroll R.	Bus, Org
Leffler, Hattie	Earlyear	Matlin, Marlee	Ed, Stage
Leigh, Irene	Ed, Med, Org	Maxwell, Sally	Sports
Leitch, Margaret	Sports	May, Florence	Stage, Art, Lit
Lenham, Sheila	Stage	Mayberry, Mercedes	Bus
Lentz, Ella Mae	Comm, Stage	Mayes, Julia Burg	Med, Ed, Stage
Lependorf, Bertt	Ack	McAndrew, Frances	Blkdeaf
Lependorf, Betty-Jo	Comm, Org	McCallon, Marilyn	Art, Lit
Lerner, Shirley	Reli	McCarty, Tim	Stage
Levenson, Randy Sue	Reli	McCrorey, Mary	Bus
Levesque, Ann	Mother	McGann, Ana	Stage
Lewis, Emily	Ed	McGee, Donna	Stage
Lewis, Nancy	Org, Ed	McKinney, J. Charlie	CommSvc
Lincoln, Abraham	Earlyear	McNab, Joyce	Org
Linstrom, Martha	Med	McNally, Debi	Org
Lockhart, Matthew	Fem	McVan, Alice	Art, Lit
Long, Gwen	Sports	Medoff, Mark	Stage
Lopez, Patty	Sports	Menken, Helen	Stage
Lorenzo, Kathy	Lit	Meyer, Marcella	Bus
Lothrop, Cornelia	Reli, Lit	Meyers, Adele	Reli
Low, Juliette Gordon	Vict, Lit, Art	Middleton, Mildred	Ed
Lowe, Rob	Stage	Miles, Dorothy	Stage, Lit, Comm
Lowman, Alto	Earlyear	Miller, Betty	Art, Comm, Ed
Luckey, Helen	Blkdeaf	Miller, Jane	Mother, Lit
Luddy, Mabel	Bus	Miller, Lucille	Ed
Ludovico, Ruth	Org	Miller, Marvin	Fem
Lund, Sandra	Reli	Miller, MaryBeth	Stage
Lundquist, Cheryl	Stage	Mitchell, Lydia	Ed
Lupo, Frances	Ed, Stage	Montague, Margaret	DeafBlind
Lynch, Joyce	Art, Stage	Montgomery, Ida	Vict
Lynch, Patsy	Sposrts, Lit	Montoya, Elaine	Art

Name	Chapter	Name	Chapter
Moore, Mary Jean	Legal, Ed	Parsons, Frances	Comm, Lit
Morden, Leona	Sports	Parsons, Hester	Lit
Morikawa, Georgia	CommSvc	Paul, Eileen	Org
Morris, Brian	Ed	Pauley, Gladys	Bus
Morris, Myrtle	Reli	Peale, Charles	Earlyear
Morse, Samuel	Vict	Pederson, Carlene	Comm
Morse, Sarah	Vict	Peet, Elizabeth	Vict, Fem
Morton, Azie	Blkdeaf	Peet, Mary Toles	Lit, Mother
Mudgett, Grace	CommSvc	Peikoff, Pauline	CommSvc
Mulrooney, Jean	Med	Peltier, Sara	Bus
Munoz, Julie	Lit	Pereira, Jacob	Earlyear, Art
Muse, Helen	Lit	Petal, Marla	Reli
Musmanno, Madeline	Ed	Petersen, Helen	Queen
		Peterson, Julie	Queen
Nagel, Virginia	Reli	Peterson, Ruth	Ack, Art, Mother
Naiman, Rachel	Ed	Philbrick, Rachel	Lit
Nash, Catherine	Bus	Phillips, Ruth	CommSvc
Nelson, Edith	Lit	Pitrois, Yvonne	Intro, Lit
Nelson, Julie	CommSvc	Plapinger, Anna	Reli
Newkirk, June	Ed	Pocobello, Donna	Ed
Nicholsom, Alice	Lit	Porter, Sarah	Mother
Noble, Mary	Queen, Org	Potter, Kathleen	DeafBlind
Noble, Roy	Queen	Pratt, Judy	Stage
Norman, Freda	Comm, Stage	Prince, of Wales	Vict
Norman, Jane	Lit, Comm, Stage	Princess, Alexandria	Vict
Northup, Helen	Lib, Ed	Princess, Pocahontas	Earlyear
Norton, Audree	Stage	Pugin, Mary	Ed
Novitsky, MaryLou	Stage	Pumphrey, Catherine	Mother
Nowak, Marcia	Org		
		Quinn, Elizabeth	Stage
O'Grady, Cindy	Comm		
O'Grady, Maureen	Comm	Radar, Ruby	Lit
Oliva, Gina	CommSrv	Rainey, Nelda	Bus
O'Neill, Kitty	Sports	Rarus, Tim	Mother
Orleck-Aiello, Myrna	Bus	Rasmus, Carola	Comm
Orman, Doris	Ed	Rasmus, Ray	Comm
Orman, James	Ed	Ratto, Aurelia	Org
Oshman, Betty	Reli	Reagan, Nancy	CommSvc
		Reagan, Ronald	Ed, Blkdeaf
Pachiarz, Judith	Ed, Sports	Reed, Ruth	Blkdeaf
Padden, Agnes	Ack	Reedy, Charity	Stage
Padden, Carol	Comm, Ed	Reins, Donetta	Fem
Padden, Melinda	Org	Rems, Julie	Queen
Pakula, Dorothy	Reli	Reneau, Alvah	CommSvc
Panara, John	Lit	Rennie, Debbie	Comm, Art
Panara, Robert	Lit	Rhodes, Annie	Mother
Panara, Shirley	Lit	Richmond, Fred	Blkdeaf
Parmenter, Christine	Lit	Rikuris, Edith	Ed

Name	Chapter	Name	Chapter
Rinaldi, Anna	Org	Sharpless, Nansie	Fem, Ed
Risser, Linda	Lit	Sheiber, Loel F.	Lit
Ritter, Deirdre	Ed, Honors	Shelton, Jane Ann	Org
Ritter, William	Blkdeaf	Sheridan, Laura	Fem
Roberts, Ruth	Med	Sherman, Margaret	Earlyear
Rocheleau, Corinne	Lit	Shook, Nancy B. R.	Fem, Mother
Rocque, Gwen	Sports	Shores, Patricia	Ed
Rogers, Clara Bella	Org, Vict	Shuart, Adele	Stage, Reli
Rosen, Jeff	Mother	Siegel, Celia	Reli
Rosen, Roslyn	Ack, Ed, Fem	Sigorney, Lydia	Earlyear
Rosenstein, Rebecca	Reli	Sills, Beverly	Stage
Rosiecki, Patricia	Sports	Silver, Ann	Art
Roth, Ellen	Stage, Art, Org	Silver, Toby	Stage
Roth, Jacqueline	Queen	Simmons, Lionel	Fem
Rothenberg, June	Ed	Simpson, Mikki	Org
Rowley, Amy	Lit, Bus	Singleton, Bernice	Org
Rowley, Clifford	Bus	Skinner, Lillian	CommSvc, Sports
Rowley, Nancy	Bus, Lit	Skinner, Ruth	CommSvc, Bus
Rozynek, Yola	Stage	Skinner, Virginia	Sports
Rudd, Ellen	Earlyear	Skyer, Solange	Org
Russell, Kathleen	Sports	Sloan, Tarhonda	Fem
Russo, Joanne	Fem	Sloane, Jeanette	Org
Ryan, Bonnie	Ed	Smith, Adelaide	Ed
		Smith, Alberta	CommSrv
Sabrins, Florence	CommSvc	Smith, John	Earlyear
Saltzman, Cynthia	Stage	Smith, Marie	Sports
Samples, Ruby	Ed	Smithdas, Michelle	DeafBlind, Lit
Samuel, Kathleen	Ed	Smithdas, Robert	DeafBlind
Sanders, Mrs. Geo	Stage	Smits, Ausma	Ack, Ed
Sartain, Ida	Ed	Soll, Alice	Reli
Sassen, Marianne	Ed	Sonnenstrahl, Deborah	Art, Ed, Blkdeaf, Stage
Savanick, Ferne	Reli	Spanbauer, Pauline	Ed
Sayer, Maggie	Art	Speak, Emma	Ed
Schemenauer, Kelly	Sports	Speaks, Gwendolyn	Org
Schmidt, Nancy L.	Mother	Speck, Sharon	Med
Schornstein, Ruth Ann	Bus	Speer, Kathleen	DeafBlind
Schreiber, Kathleen	Lit, Ack, Stage	St. John, Peggy	Fem
Schrodel, Huberta	Bus	Stack, Linda	Ed
Schuer, Mary	Med	Stecker, Arlene	Stage
Schultz, Ursula	CommSvc	Steinberg, Robert	Stage
Schuster, Monica	Comm	Stern, Carolyn	Ed
Schwartzman, Dot	Mother	Stern, Hedy U.	Mother, Stage
Scroggin, Bobbie	Stage	Stern, Ruth	Reli
Sculthrope, Brandeis Ann	Queen	Stewart, Susan	Fem
Searing, Laura	Fem, Lit	Stokes, Darren	Fem
Seeger, Ruth	Sports	Stone, Jeannette	Blkdeaf
Shaffer, Elaine	Comm	Stout, Hallea	Lit
Shaffer, Ronald	Fem	Strassler, Muriel	Lit